OPENING SUMMARY	2
WELCOME NOTE	5
FIVERR EARNING POTENTIAL AND OPPORTUNITIES	8
SETTING UP YOUR FIVERR AND PAYPAL ACCOUNT	**17**
CREATE YOUR PAYPAL ACCOUNT	18
CREATE YOUR FIVERR ACCOUNT	23
SETTING UP YOUR PROFILE AND GIGS	**27**
SETTING UP YOUR PROFILE	28
SETTING UP YOUR GIG	30
STEP 1: WRITE YOUR GIG OVERVIEW	31
STEP 2: PRICE YOUR GIG	33
STEP 3: GIVE YOUR GIG A DESCRIPTION AND FAQ	36
STEP 4: ESTABLISH YOUR GIG REQUIREMENTS	37
STEP 5: ADD A GALLERY TO YOUR GIG	38
STEP 6: PUBLISH YOUR GIG	40
FIVERR LEVELS, METRICS AND COMPETITOR ANALYSIS	**41**
FIVERR LEVELS AND THEIR IMPORTANCE	41
THE IMPORTANCE OF METRICS FOR LEVELING UP ON FIVERR	49
ON FIVERR THE CUSTOMER IS ALWAYS RIGHT EVEN WHEN THEY'RE COMPLETELY WRONG	53
RESEARCH COMPETITION TO SEE WHO IS SELLING WHAT	56
HOW FIVERR IS BETTER THAN OTHER FREELANCING PLATFORMS!	**61**
OPTIMIZE YOUR GIG TO INCREASE SALES AND GET A 4 FIGURE INCOME EVERY MONTH	**68**
STEP NUMBER 1: ADD A VIDEO TO YOUR GIG	69
STEP NUMBER 2: OPTIMIZE YOUR GIG TITLE TO GET MORE NUMBER OF CLICKS	71
STEP NUMBER 3: WRITE A WINNING GIG DESCRIPTION	73
GIG EXTRAS: THEY WILL BRING YOUR REAL MONEY IN THE LONG RUN	**78**
UNIQUE STRATEGY: DRIVE MORE SALES WITH A LONGER WAITING PERIOD	**83**
HOW BUYER REVIEWS AFFECT YOUR SALES ON FIVERR	**87**
FIVERR LEVEL AND RATING SYSTEM	87
FIVERR REVIEW SYSTEM FOR BUYERS AND SELLERS	92
SIX TRIED AND TESTED WAYS TO MAINTAIN MINIMUM RATINGS AND REVIEWS ON FIVERR	94
AVOID ASKING BUYERS FOR A POSITIVE REVIEW	102
DEALING WITH CUSTOMER SUPPORT FOR A RATING YOU DO NOT AGREE WITH	104
FIVE METHODS TO MAKE YOUR FIVERR BUSINESS A ROARING SUCCESS	**107**
CONCLUDING SUMMARY	**126**

Opening Summary

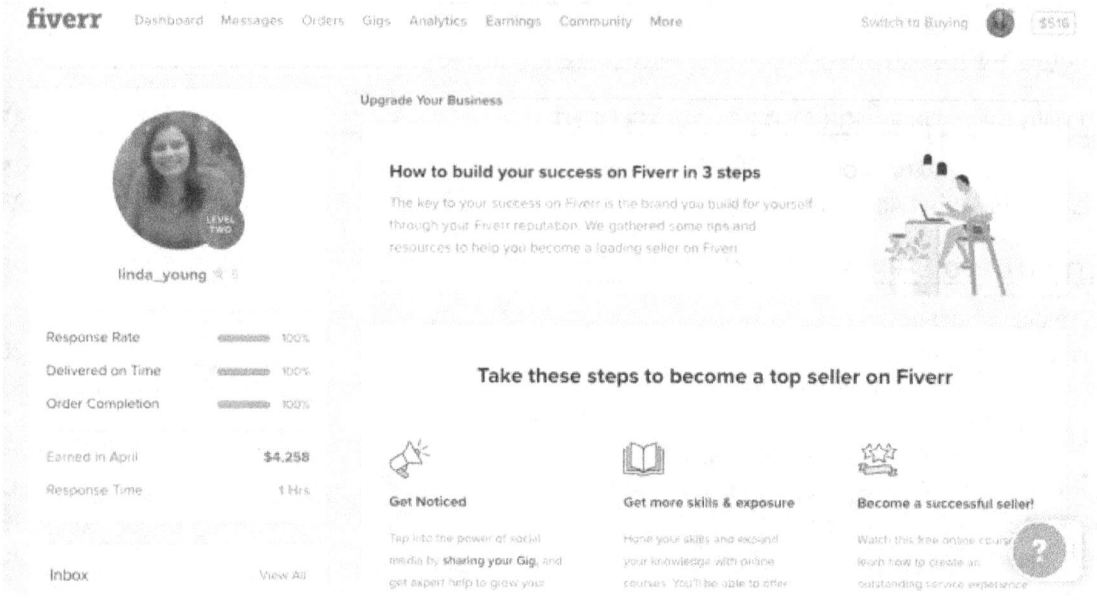

Hi I am Linda and I want to welcome you to this course. Before I delve into this any further, I will share in brief with you, my personal journey with Fiverr. I joined Fiverr in November 2016. Before joining this platform I had done a lot of research on what it takes to become a successful seller in Fiverr. At that time Fiverr wasn't very strict with their rules and regulations and based upon my research I created a few gigs, which became very successful immediately. I was soon dealing with a heavy workflow of orders and I was a little too careless by either not delivering on time or not really caring about the ratings because the income was good and steady. I was too busy in making money.

It wasn't long before orders started drying up and then Fiverr introduced strict rules and regulations, which affected my business completely. I lost all the levels that I attained so I had to start right from scratch. I redesigned my gigs, made my services more attractive and competitive and learnt how to maintain the strict metrics and leveling system to once again restore my credibility and income on Fiverr. I also organized my personal life and work schedule so that I could deliver my projects on time. The journey so far has been exciting and exhilarating with its fair share of ups and downs and I am enjoying every minute of it.

I shared my experiences with a lot of friends who themselves are in the freelancing business. Based upon my tips and feedback, they became quite successful in their areas of freelancing work. That's when I thought; let me create an eBook first and maybe a tutorial video later. I took the time out of my (already overburdened) schedule to create this eBook so that I can not only have means to earn a passive income for myself but to also help other freelancers who are struggling to make it out there. It took me three months to put together this eBook. I have only worked with Fiverr so this book is based entirely on how to become a successful seller on Fiverr.

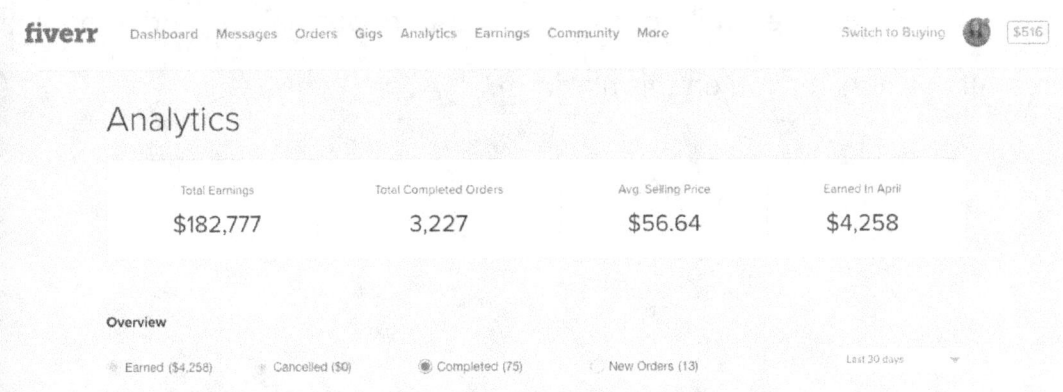

Please take a look at the screenshot above. This is the earning potential you can create for yourself. It's no rocket science; there are no complex formulas involved, just a basic understanding of what not to do and what to do and that too effectively.

Successful freelancers hardly complain and whine, they suffer setbacks like anybody else but they take it in their stride and move on. I have had situations where I lost thousands of bucks due to buyers cancelling orders for no fault of mine. Didn't matter, I worked on other orders to keep my income flow steady. If I could do this, you too can do it. I not only worked hard on my gigs but also raised my skill sets (in video editing and creation) so that I could create more successful gigs on Fiverr.

So far I have 12 running gigs with the option of adding 8 more gigs (as my level allows 20 gigs). Out of 12, 8 gigs have services which I can deliver in 1-2 hours but I have deliberately kept the delivery period to 3 days or more. We will talk about this more in a detailed lesson. So here is the first tip of this course; "Create certain gigs that are extremely easy for you to deliver and price them accordingly". Along with working hard, you also need to work smart if you want to make serious money on Fiverr. There are so many opportunities on Fiverr, use this course well to explore those opportunities and create a successful business for you on this platform.

Chapter 1

Welcome Note

I want to take a moment to thank you for joining my course. Fiverr is one of the largest online marketplaces for freelancers. They have become pioneers in the freelance market with this unique idea of selling services for just $5. Right now you can start your career on Fiverr, the right way is by using proven strategies that are employed by the most successful sellers on Fiverr. In this course I'm going to show you how to become a level 2 or top rated seller in Fiverr and earn a four figure income every month.

As I mentioned Fiverr is a global online marketplace offering various tasks and services beginning at a cost of five dollars per job performed. This is how Fiverr derived its name. It always starts with a five-dollar job. If you ever wonder that how a five dollar job can earn you massive income, well, keep reading, you will get to know how.

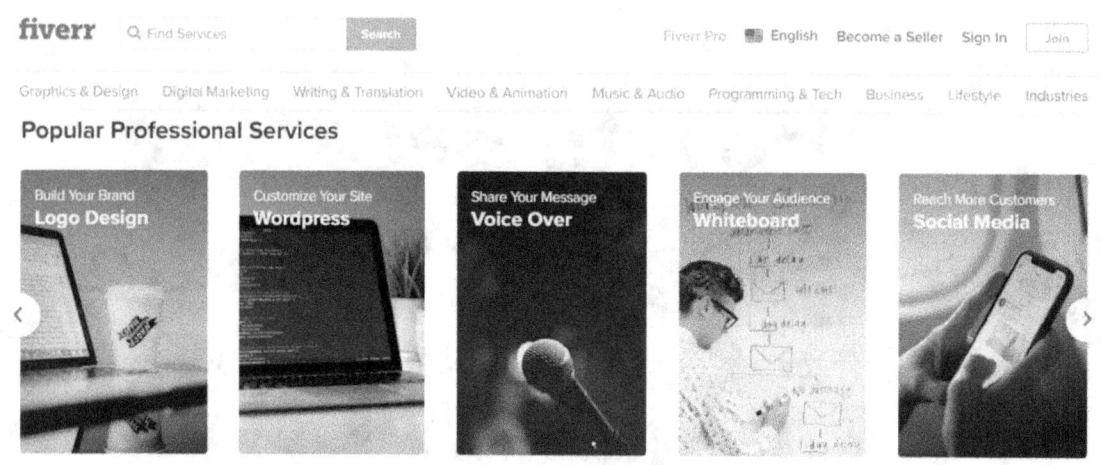

Fiverr is extremely easy to navigate and use. The website design is clean and clear that even first-timers can understand the concept easily and in no time at all. The buyers and sellers don't need to hassle themselves with contracts or agreements. The buyers can simply place an order and don't need to worry about invoicing or other project logistics. An account on Fiverr is all you need to start with, whether you are a seller or a buyer. The concept of selling on Fiverr is straightforward. You need to follow this three step procedure:

1. Communicate with a buyer
2. Accept the gig or send them a custom offer
3. Deliver the gig and complete the order.

The fact that Fiverr has such a huge global outreach; it gives the seller an unlimited earning potential. Your money is safe because the customer pays upfront when the order is placed. This payment is held by Fiverr until the service is completed by the seller. You get rid of the hassle of chasing clients to get paid for your work. Payments with Fiverr are secure and you're also protected from any kind of credit card fraud. The more business you do on Fiverr, the more visibility you will get in its marketplace.

With a few simple steps you can make money while doing something that you love. Wouldn't you like to achieve this goal for yourself? You can do this if you play your cards right. In the next chapter we will discuss the earning potential and opportunities offered at Fiverr.

Chapter 2

Fiverr earning potential and opportunities

We've already talked about how Fiverr can be a great source of income online and it is also a platform for freelancers that offer a multitude of services (or "gigs") in contact with buyers looking to outsource a task. It covers more or less every category of digital service that you can think of. This is why Fiverr has become an incredibly attractive place for those looking for digital services. Luckily for us, this also means that Fiverr is accommodating of a plethora of skills. This can range from logo designing, building a website or even just impersonating celebrities! So what this means for us is that we can make money right now or develop our skills and make more potential money in the future.

If you are just starting out in the realm of earning money online, Fiverr could be considered one of the best places to start. Thanks to its recent brand campaigns, 'Fiverr' is now becoming a household name and what's more, businesses have started to get in on it, meaning that it has become the largest marketplace online for micro-services. If the ability to draw fresh clients daily is enough to convince you, its sheer diversity of services means you can likely monetize yourself right now.

People joining Fiverr fall under two categories; skilled and non-skilled. While the former category can easily set up and monetize their service, the latter needs to put in a little more work while setting up their service. This should not however discourage those without skills as it is easily possible to develop them within a short space of time.

It's important to know this one point before starting out in the freelance market. Most freelancers make a common mistake of looking at a service that is making the most money and then running through with it. However this isn't a logical starting point because if you have marketable skills already, you need to work with your strengths first. If you want instant results, and if you are just starting out with no existing marketable skills, the likelihood of being able to compete effectively in large competitive markets is very low.

For example, Animation is the biggest market out there now and so if you already know the technical skills involved in animation then great! But if you're just starting out, then it would be a better use of your time to pick a more accessible niche or alternatively, you can enter the competitive niche but instead become specialized within it so that you rank in a niche that's within a bigger niche.

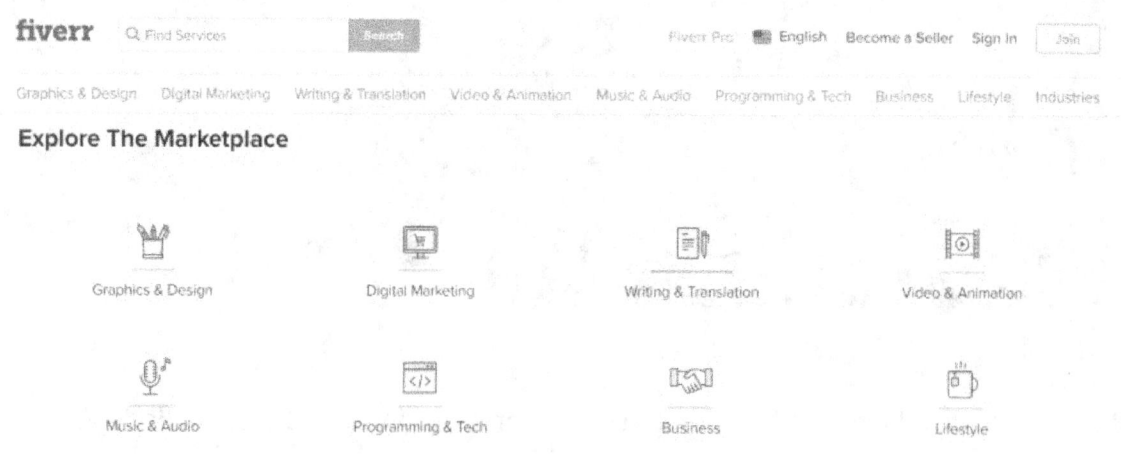

As we've discussed, there are Fiverr jobs for almost every kind of skill and talent. In fact, there are over 200 different job categories on the site! Here are just of few of the best ways to make money on Fiverr.

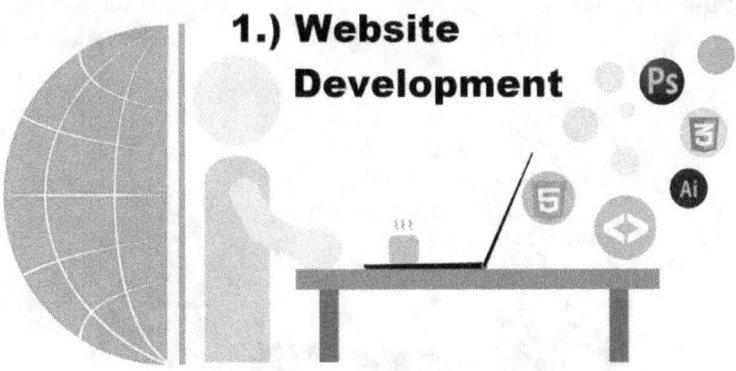

Designing and building a website is arguably one of the highest-paid jobs on Fiverr. You can easily earn $100 to $2,000 per gig under this service. Although you'll find different offers for website concept, design, and coding, you'll make more money if you are able to do all three. Particularly, e-commerce web design is in high demand. Buyers are specifically looking for sellers who can build on platforms such as WordPress, Squarespace, and Shopify.

On Fiverr, there is no shortage of graphic design offers available. It remains one of the most popular categories on the site, with over 11,000 available gigs. This service offers a payout of $10 to $1000 per gig. Whether you specialize in T-shirt, logo, or business card design, you shouldn't have a problem finding a graphic design gig on Fiverr.

Another lucrative gig is copywriting. You don't have to be a tech wiz to make money on Fiverr! If you're a wordsmith, you too can earn extra money by offering your copywriting services to buyers. Under this service you can make $50 to $2000 per gig. There are plenty of writing gigs available, especially when it comes to copywriting. For example, you will find listings that pay product review writers, bloggers, and even eBook authors.

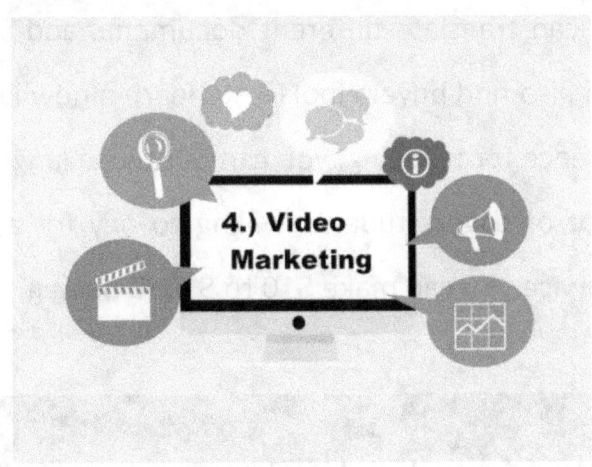

Video marketing is one of the highest paying services across all types of Fiverr gig. I too have listed 12 gigs in Fiverr under this category. Over the last few years, the demand for these types of services has grown exponentially, which makes it a lucrative option for those with video experience. Options include training videos, short animations, and advertisements. There's also a big market for businesses trying to grow their social media efforts. You'll find gigs looking for YouTube, Instagram, and Facebook video services. This service offers payouts from $10 to $10000 per gig.

If you can speak more than one language, you can easily make extra cash by translating documents for others. Businesses are eagerly looking for multilingual sellers who can translate different documents and articles. Along the same lines, you can also find buyers looking to learn a new language on Fiverr. If you have the patience for teaching, you can put those language skills to good use. There are a lot of eager students willing to pay for a private language tutor. Under this service you can make $10 to $1000 per gig.

Voice over work is a popular service which offers a payout of $5 to $500 per gig. It is lucrative gig even for those without a lot of experience. All you need is a clear speaking voice and you can create your own gig. Believe me, there are tons of gigs on Fiverr for every type of voice. American accent, British accent, male, female, you name it.

7.) Illustration

Whether you're a pro at drawing comics or just like dabbling with caricatures as a hobby, Fiverr is a great way to find different illustration gigs. Most of the gigs will need to be customized, as businesses are usually looking for unique characters, cartoons, or portraits. The payout in this service is $5 to $300 per gig.

8.) Virtual Assistant

Becoming a virtual assistant allows you to work from anywhere you want in the world! If you're good at staying organized and managing multiple schedules, working as a virtual assistant is a good option. Fiverr has a seemingly endless supply of virtual assistant jobs. Tasks include data entry, appointment setting, and cold calling. This is one category that is constantly in high demand. You can make $5 to $100 per gig under this service.

So I guess we've covered quite a few earning opportunities in Fiverr. With the right skills, dedication, and a positive work ethic, you can easily create online gigs that fit your talent and lifestyle.

Once you've built your reputation on Fiverr you will see and experience for yourself how easy it is to make money over here. With some dedication, it's entirely possible to make good money and fund your world travels. You'll have the potential to earn as much as you can while having the freedom to work wherever you want.

By choosing what gigs you want, you can dictate the hours you work to fit around your schedule, making it the perfect option for that side hustle or digital nomad lifestyle. And trust us, you can't say that about too many other jobs on the market right now. In the next lesson, we will go through the process of setting up your Fiverr as well as Paypal account.

Chapter 3

Setting up your Fiverr and Paypal Account

Now that I have familiarized you with the whole concept of what Fiverr can do for you, the next step is to prepare the necessary tools for it. First of all you will need to sign up for a Fiverr account. The process of signing up is simple. Just enter your email and set up your password. Do your own niche research. Looking for a suitable niche to start the business is the utmost important task you should do before anything else. It can be something which you are already doing what you love and most importantly something that can sell.

Create your Paypal Account

It is always good to have your own PayPal account before signing up with Fiverr. PayPal is the main payment method that is accepted by Fiverr. If you already own one, link it to your Fiverr account. If you do not have one it's time to create one. Do not worry about the fee as creating a PayPal account is free. In this chapter I will guide you step by step on how to set up your PayPal account.

Step 1

Visit the PayPal website. You can create an account from the PayPal homepage. Click "Sign Up for Free". This will begin the account creation process. For business accounts, there are two different options, each of which has a different cost structure and benefits. Sign up for the "Standard account", it is free. You really do not need to sign up for a pro account because it's not needed at this stage. The Standard free business account is best suited for users who have started freelancing on Fiverr.

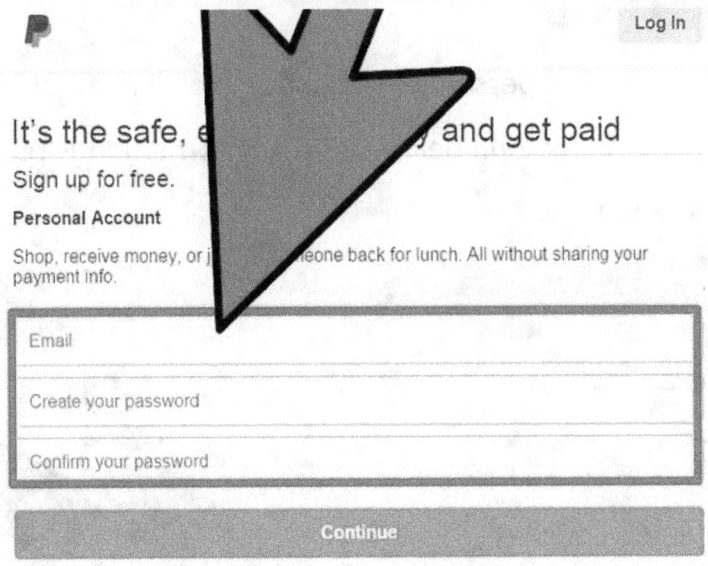

Step 2

Enter your email address and create a password. Make sure that you create a strong password so that nobody else can access your financial information. Enter a valid email address because you'll need to use it to verify your account.

Step 3

Fill out the form with your personal information. You'll need to enter your legal name, address, and phone number. All of this information is required in order to create your account.

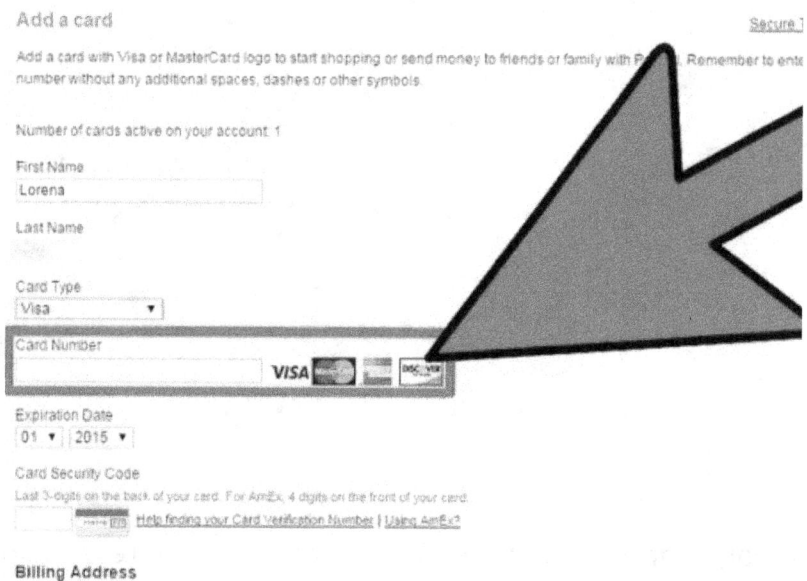

Step 4

After entering your personal information, you'll be prompted to enter your credit or debit card. If you are not going to make any purchases through PayPal, you need not enter your card details. You can enter this now or later, but you'll need to at some point if you want to verify your PayPal account.

If you don't want to enter your card information now, click "I'd rather link my bank first".

Step 5

Enter your bank account information. This is important because you'll need a bank account linked if you plan on receiving money and want to be able to transfer it to your bank. Make sure to enter your bank account details before you move on to the next step.

Step 6

Before you're taken to your account's Summary page, PayPal will prompt you to sign up for a line of credit. Again, this is not needed for you at this stage. Click "No thanks" and move on to the next step.

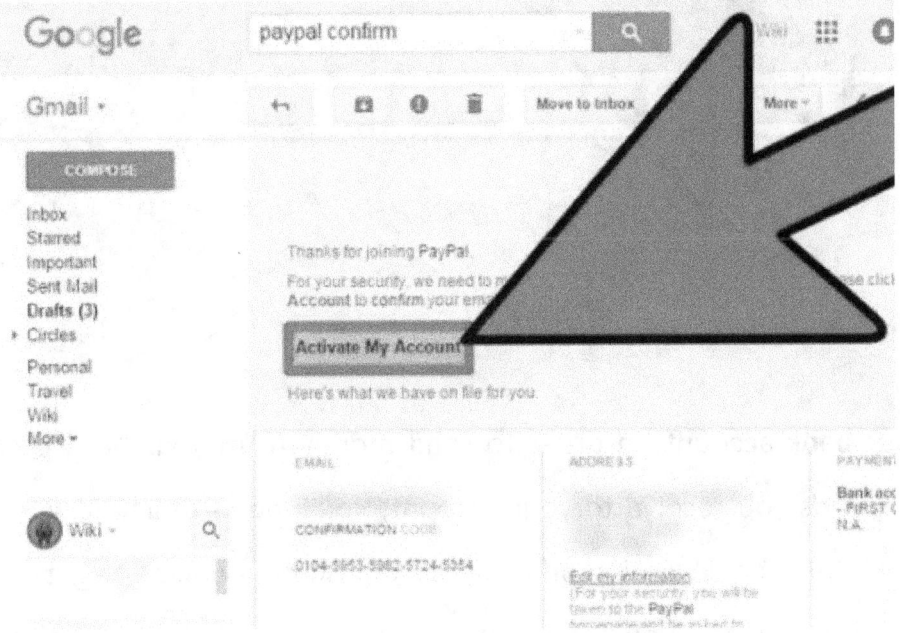

Step 7

Verify your account by confirming your email address. In order to receive money at your PayPal account, you'll need to confirm your email address. You will receive an email once you created your account. Click the "Yes, this is my email" button in the email message to confirm your email address. If you can't find the message, check your Spam or Junk folder in your email. You can have PayPal send another message from your account Summary page. Click "Confirm Email" to send another message.

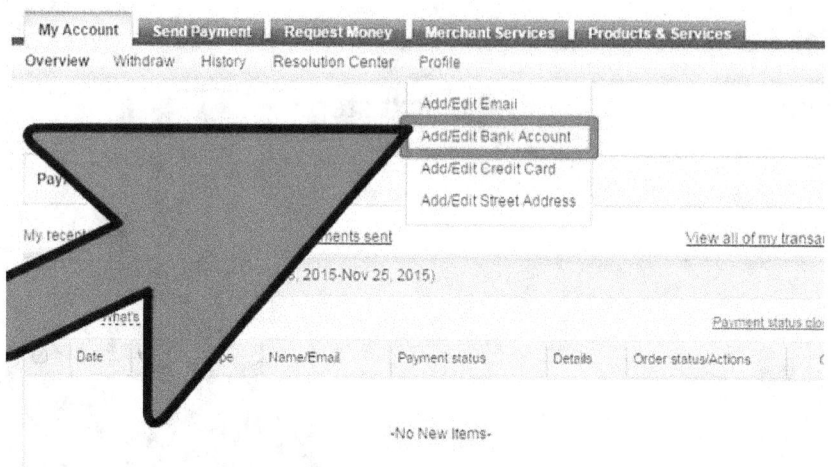

Step 8

Link your bank account. In order to send money from your bank account or transfer funds you receive to your account, you'll need to link it with PayPal. Click the "Link a bank" option on your account Summary page to get started. If your bank is listed, you'll be able to enter your online banking login information to automatically link your account.

If your bank is not listed, you'll need to enter your account number and routing number. You can find these on the bottom of your checks. This will take a day or two to confirm. PayPal will make two small deposits into your account, totaling less than a dollar. You'll need to enter these two values in order to confirm that you are the owner of the bank account. You'll be able to find these deposits on your online statement after 24-48 hours.

Create your Fiverr Account

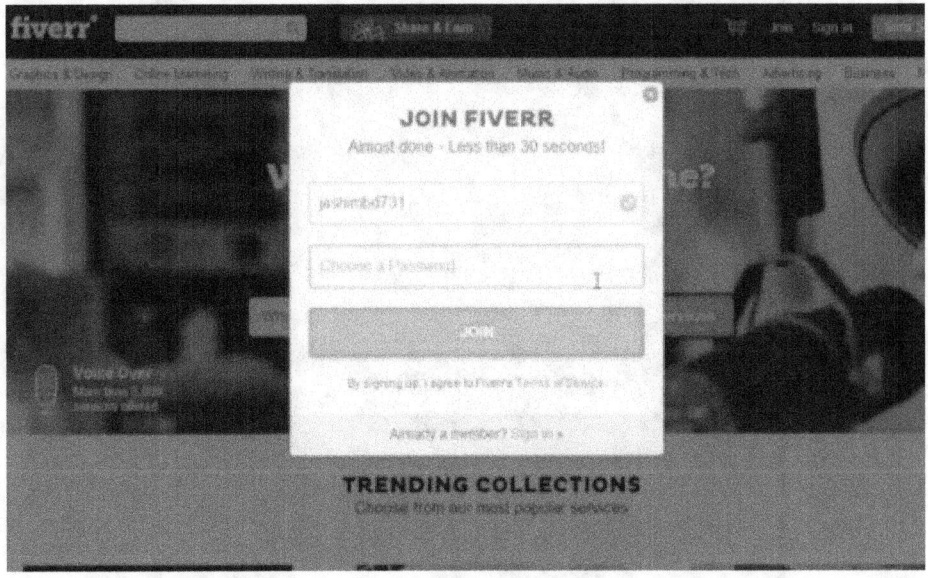

Now that you own a Paypal account, it is time for you to set up your Fiverr account. First of all signing up for a Fiverr account is very easy and free of charge. Go to their website then click on join to sign up for your account. As mentioned enter your email and set up the password. Other than that you can connect Fiverr to your Facebook or Google account without creating a new account. However, before you start setting up your Fiverr account, the one thing that is very important is for you to choose the most appropriate user name.

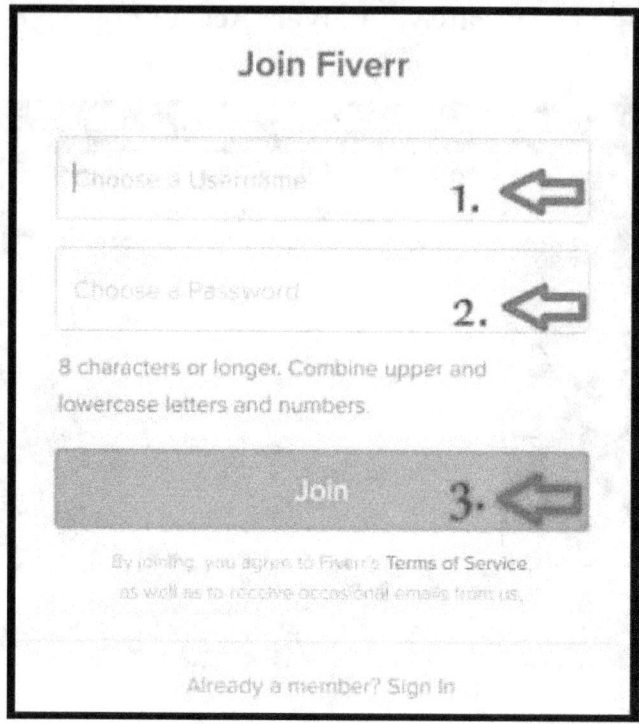

Choosing your Fiverr username is an important step that you want to get right from the start. This is because you CANNOT change your username once your account is registered. So my advice is really to just use your actual name as your username. There's a reason why I am asking you to do that. The number one reason is that your name can be linked to all your social media accounts and it will maintain a certain consistency while you are promoting yourself on social media. Secondly buyers connect well to people with real names because the conversation becomes more personalized thus hereby increasing the chances of converting the lead into a sale.

You may also want to try out different niches on Fiverr which will have their own separate gigs under different categories. So let us say for example you pick a user name of "filmcritic_Joy" because you have created a gig of reviewing films. Your gig becomes successful and you want to expand your skill into reviewing books, music, documentaries etc. So now while creating these new gigs, your username will continue to show "filmcritic_Joy" even though you want to market your "book review" gig.

This can cause a lot of confusion for buyers so there's really no advantage in this. Your new gig may fail to take off right from the start. So my advice is to use your real name so that it is consistent for all your gigs on Fiverr as well as your online profile.

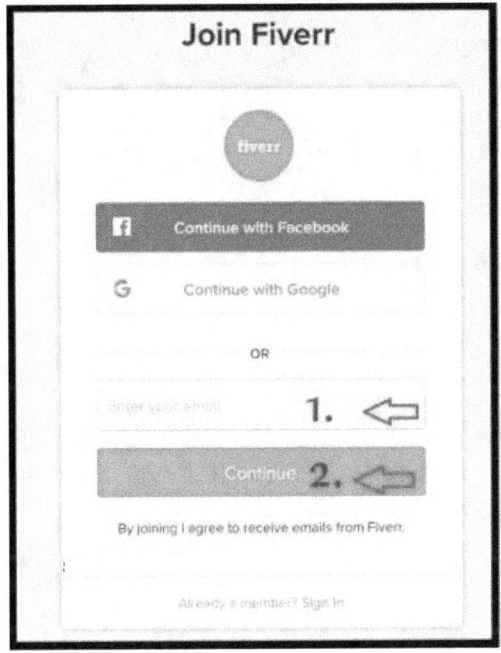

Now that you have decided what your username is, go to the Fiverr home page. Over there, click on the "Become a Seller" tab. Enter your email address and click Continue. You can also join with Facebook and Google Connect. Choose and enter you username. Your username is your display name (within your Fiverr URL), so choose it wisely. Create and enter your password and click "Join". You are now a registered user on Fiverr. An email will be sent for you to activate your account. Within the email click "Activate Your Account". That's it you are done. Congratulations, you are now a registered freelancer on Fiverr with your own PayPal account. In the next lesson, we will go through the process of setting up your gig.

Chapter 4

Setting up your profile and gigs

Setting up your profile as well as your first gig is a whole lot of fun. From graphic design to web development, personalized relationship advice to funny birthday videos, you can find pretty much any service imaginable on Fiverr. A bit different from other freelancing platforms, workers on Fiverr post their services, which clients can then browse and buy; these are called "gigs."

Important! Before you create your first gig, you should first experience how a buyer sees gigs on Fiverr. Only then you will be able to understand how to create a gig that stands out from the rest of the gigs. Buy someone else's in a gig on Fiverr. It will only cost you $7 ($5 + $2) and you can buy something you need; for example, you can buy a Fiverr image gig to make you look professional or buy a gig in which someone will proofread your gig content so that there are no mistakes. When you will go through the process of buying a Fiverr gig, you will get a deeper understanding of the buyer sentiment as well as that of how the seller has dealt with you when you made a transaction on

Fiverr. This includes crucial things such as how a buyer looks at thumbnail images to choose which gigs to try, how is the price displayed and even how the ordering process works. This will help you to set up your gig in a way to make it look attractive to your customers AND make the process of buying your gig simple one. Let us now go ahead and set up your profile.

Setting up your Profile

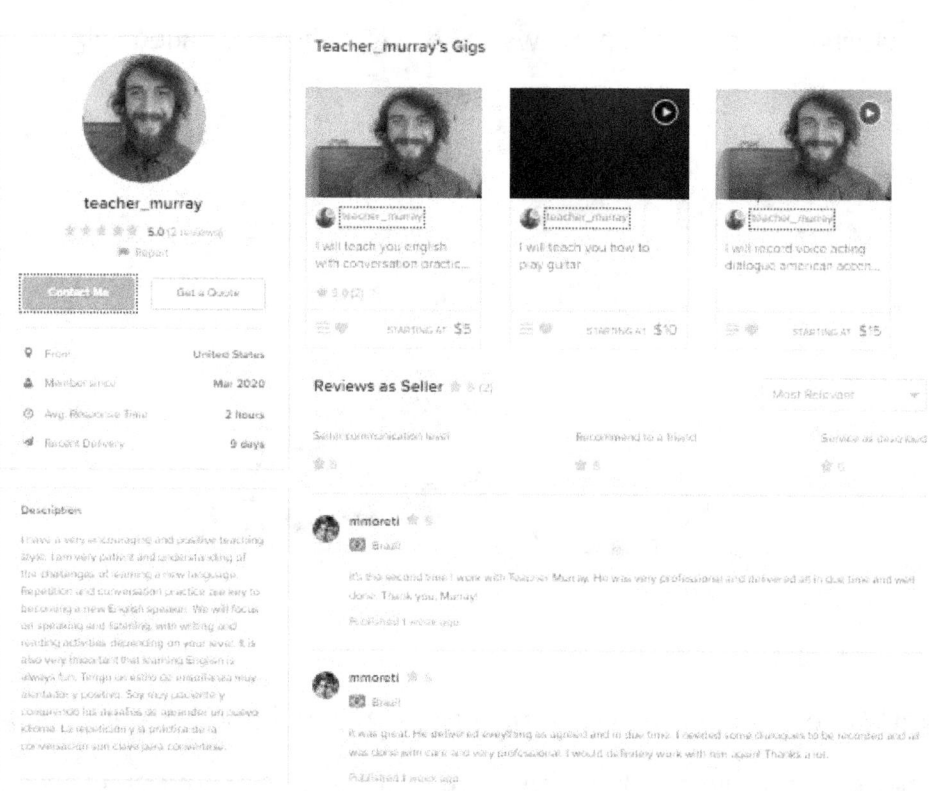

The first thing most buyers check before paying for your gig, is your profile. Fiverr will ask you to include a photo in your profile and several key pieces of information, allowing potential buyers to get to know you a bit more.

Make sure that you create a profile that delivers on each and every aspect: Include a professional looking photo of your real face. This will help to ensure that potential buyers trust that you're a real person, in addition to making your profile appear more professional.

Description: Use this section to introduce yourself to prospective buyers. Here, you can include your areas of expertise, experiences, or anything else you think is important, keep it relevant!

Languages: Let buyers know what languages you speak and your level of fluency; this is incredibly important if your gig includes skills like writing or translating. You can immediately engage with customers suited to communicate with you. Show them that you speak their language.

Tests Taken: This part of your profile will display the tests that you've taken through Fiverr. Tests help to verify your skills, and can increase a potential buyer's trust. Just be careful, as you're only able to take a test twice every three months; however, Fiverr does give you the option to hide your tests scores if you do poorly.

Skills: Here, you should include any skills applicable to the gigs you intend to create. These include abilities you've gained through past jobs, hobbies, or other life experiences. Fiverr only allows ten, so choose wisely.

Education: Include where you attended college and your degrees.

Certifications: List any additional certifications that may help you stand out from the crowd.

Link your social media accounts too. This is the biggest way you can show authenticity.

Setting up your gig

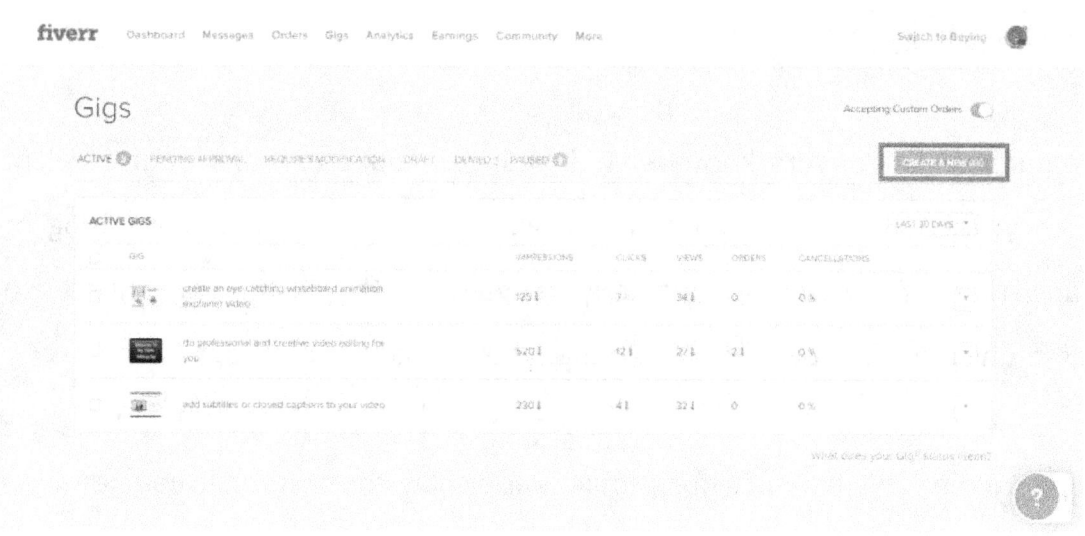

Now that your profile is set up, you can begin creating your first gig! To do this, go to the "Selling" menu at the top of the screen and in the drop-down menu choose the "Gigs" option. From here, you simply need to click the "Create New Gig" button to start the process.

Step 1: Write Your Gig Overview

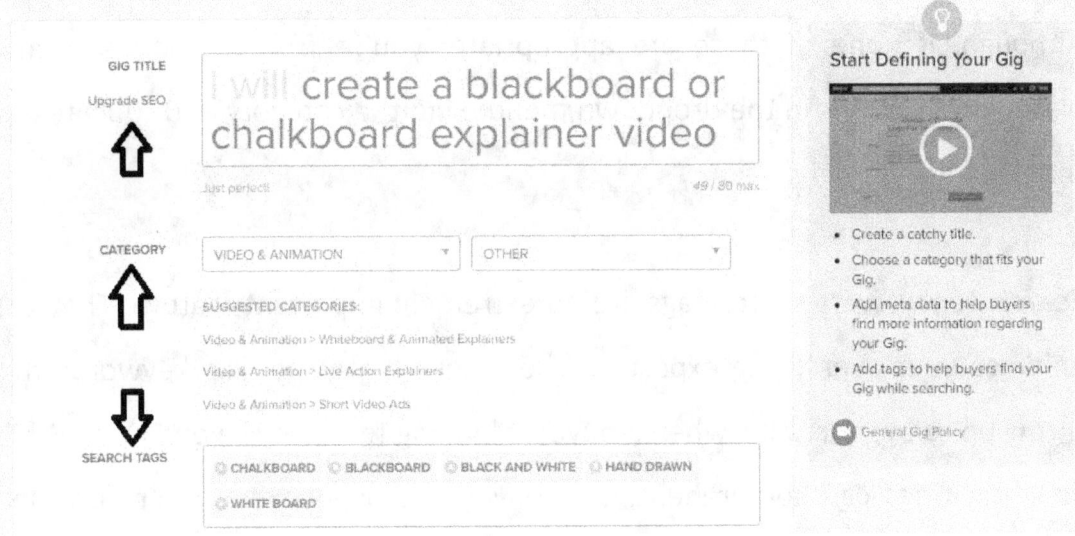

So what is a gig? What is your understanding of a gig?

Well, a gig is your "specific service offering". It is the face of your business and it should tell a customer whether or not you're a perfect seller for them at that moment. So in this section you'll need to complete the Gig Overview. Here, you'll be required to fill out three boxes:

The title of your gig

The category that it falls under

Relevant search tags

Gig Title: You're only allotted 80 characters, so make them count, and ensure that it's clear and concise; you want your prospective buyers to know exactly what it is that you're offering. Also, write something that'll stand out from the crowd by keeping the title relatively original.

Category: Based upon your title, Fiverr will automatically suggest a few categories and subcategories, and typically one will match your offering. Although, if none of these are appropriate, you're free to choose from a plethora of options in the dropdown menu. Find the category and subcategory that best fits your gig.

Search Tags: Fiverr search tags are an extremely important feature. They can enhance your overall Gig exposure. These search tags act like keywords that throw up relevant results when a buyer is looking for a service on Fiverr. While your Gig titles can comprehensively convey the buyer what you're offering, you need some extra opportunities to define your specialties. For example, you're providing article writing services on Fiverr with an expertise in sports niche. You might write the Gig title, "I will write a sports article". However, in this process you will lose all those buyers looking for articles on other niches.

So, where the title gives a chance of giving the general idea of your services, the tags help you go one step further. As in the above example, you were required to cover the whole article niches with the sports as your special one. In that case, you could write your title as, "I will an article for you", and use "sports articles" in the search tags. But how we can find best tags for our Gigs?

The sellers can find the best tags for the gigs using the Fiverr search engine. As you can see in the above picture when we ask for article services on Fiverr, the auto-complete suggests some related keywords that the buyers are frequently searching; these are the best examples of tags on Fiverr. You can use these terms in the search tags in order to grab more buyers.

Fiverr allows a maximum of five tags to use in your Gig. In order to beat your competitors, you should use four tags that buyers search frequently. The 5th tag should be unique out of the lot only intended for your gig. No doubt, this tag will find lesser exposures but will give you a sure shot sale when searched.

Once complete; click on the large green "Save and Continue" button along the bottom right of the screen to advance to the next section.

Step 2: Price Your Gig

Packages	BASIC	STANDARD	PREMIUM
	BASIC	STANDARD	PREMIUM
	30 seconds chalkboard video, fully HD	1 min video Full HD with Voice over (only sync, no recording)	2 min video Full HD with Voice over (only sync, no recording)
	2 Days Delivery	3 Days Delivery	4 Days Delivery
Revisions	1	2	2
Running Time (Seconds)	30	60	120
Full HD (1080p)			

Fiverr currently allows sellers to price their gigs in three different packages:

Basic

Standard

Premium

When filling out the scope and pricing section, there are some important things to keep in mind:

Number of Packages: It's not necessary for you to use all three packages, although many buyers do like additional premium options, so offer them where possible. Additionally, according to Fiverr, those that offer triple gig packages can earn up to 64% more per order.

Name Your Package: Choose an eye-catching title for each of your packages, and make certain that the difference between them is crystal clear.

Package Description: Briefly explain what's included in each package, and why you've included it. You're only allowed 100 characters here, so you may have to get creative to fit in everything you'd like to say. Just make sure the offerings are clear to any potential buyers.

Delivery Time: How long you'll take to complete a project. Depending on the scope of the work, this may vary greatly between packages.

Revisions: The number of times you'll alter your work upon the buyer's request. Premium packages often include additional revisions.

Price: Each package can be priced anywhere from $5 to $995 USD. Your basic package should always be priced lowest, and your premium the highest. Remember, you can always change your price later, so in the beginning, it may be smart to keep them low to help build reviews.

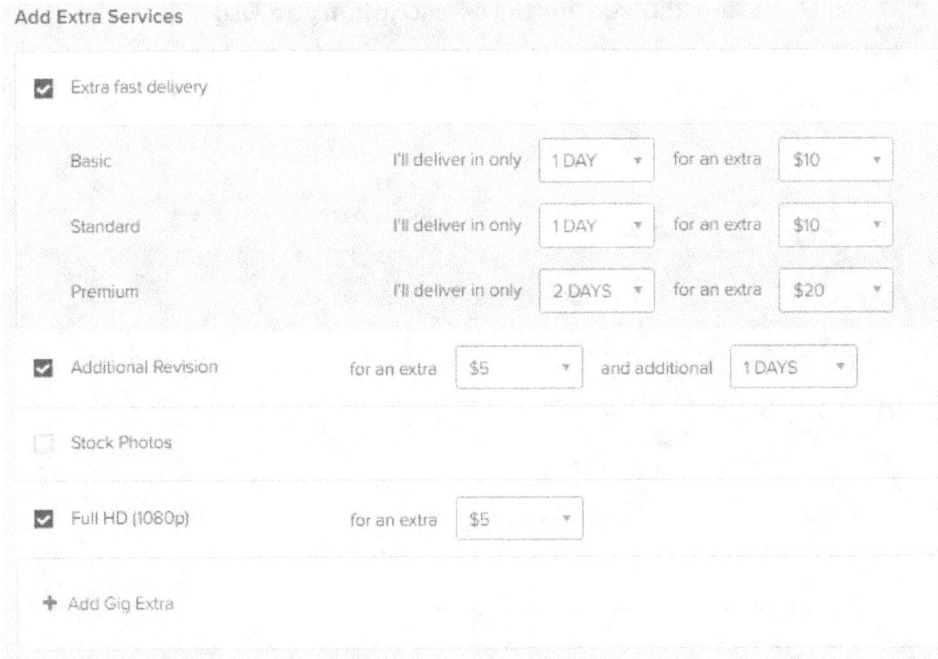

My Gig Extras: Here, you can charge additional fees for whatever extras you'd like to add to your packages. There are some frequently used extras that can be chosen from a menu, such as extra fast delivery and additional revisions. If there's an extra you'd like to include but isn't available, Fiverr makes it easy to create your own. Simply click the "Add Gig Extra" option at the bottom of "My Gig Extras" and fill out its title, description, and price.

Shipping: Fill in a shipping charge if you're going to be sending a tangible product and require compensation. You're given the option to choose multiple prices depending on the location.

Step 3: Give Your Gig a Description and FAQ

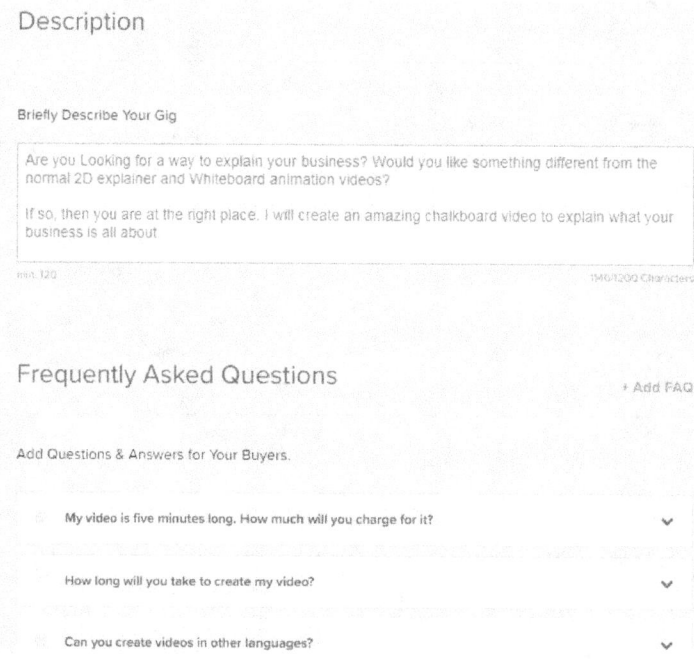

Along with your title, the description is one of the most important aspects of creating a gig that will land you clients.

Here, you're expected to go into great detail about your offer. For this reason, there's a 120 character minimum, and a 1200 character maximum for the description. Don't leave any important details out as your buyers should have an accurate enough description to determine whether or not what you're offering will satisfy their needs.

Do not be vague; be crystal clear on what you are offering. You don't want unhappy clients leaving negative feedback on your timeline. These will potentially destroying future opportunities for you on this platform.

Once your description is completed, the frequently asked questions (FAQ) will come next. In this section, provide the answers to questions you'd expect to receive relevant to your gig. This will probably need to be revised later, as you may not know what many of your FAQ will be until after your gig has been active for some time. Click the "Add FAQ" button to include as many FAQ as needed.

Step 4: Establish Your Gig Requirements

This is where you'll include any requirements that are necessary for your buyer to supply in order for you to complete the job. You're given three different methods of asking for this information, including:

Free Text: With free text, you write in your requirements, and the buyer is expected to fulfill them with a text message response.

Multiple Answers: This option allows you to ask a question and give multiple answer choices from which your buyer can choose. You need a minimum of two answers to choose from, and can add more simply by clicking the " Add Optional Answer" button.

Attached File: If you require a file from your buyer in order to complete your work, choose this option. You need to specify what this file should include in the description window, and your buyer will be asked to upload it upon purchase.

You can add as many requirements as necessary by clicking the "+Add Another Requirement" button that appears upon submission of your first. If the answer to a requirement is optional, you should unclick the "Answer is Mandatory" box.

Step 5: Add a Gallery to Your Gig

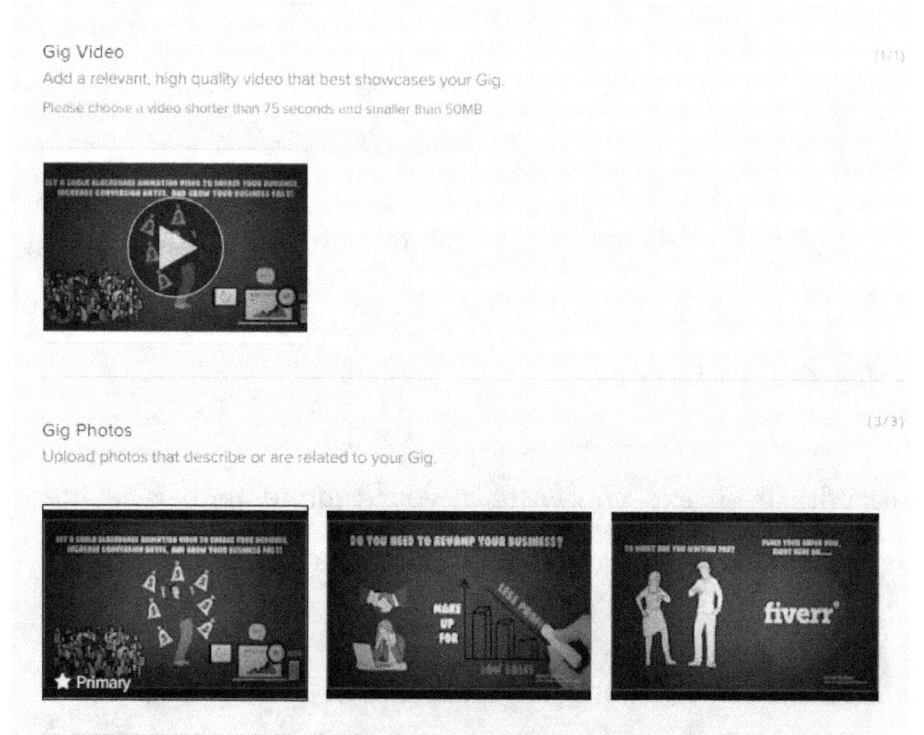

Your gig gallery can either be comprised of photos, a video, PDFs, or all of the above. The files you choose to put in your gallery should all be relevant to your gig's offerings.

Gig Photos: Most listings will include a photo that's relevant to the service being sold, especially if it's a graphic or web design gig. Even if the job is something that's not easily photographed, such as a writing gig, still include a photo. Just choose something relevant to the job, even if it's not necessarily a work sample. Fiverr allows up to three photos that can be shown in your gallery. Make sure your images are free from plagiarism; otherwise your gig may not be approved.

Gig Videos: Other than gigs in the animation and video categories, adding a gig video is optional, although they can be helpful. According to Fiverr, gigs that include a video receive up to 200% more orders, as well as enjoy 40% higher user engagement levels. Videos cannot exceed 75 seconds in length, nor can they include personal contacts.

Gig PDFs: These should only be used when further clarification is needed, and a PDF is the best format for accomplishing this. This option is generally reserved for writers, and others whose work examples are most likely to be in a PDF text format. Fiverr allows for two PDFs to be attached to each gallery.

Step 6: Publish Your Gig

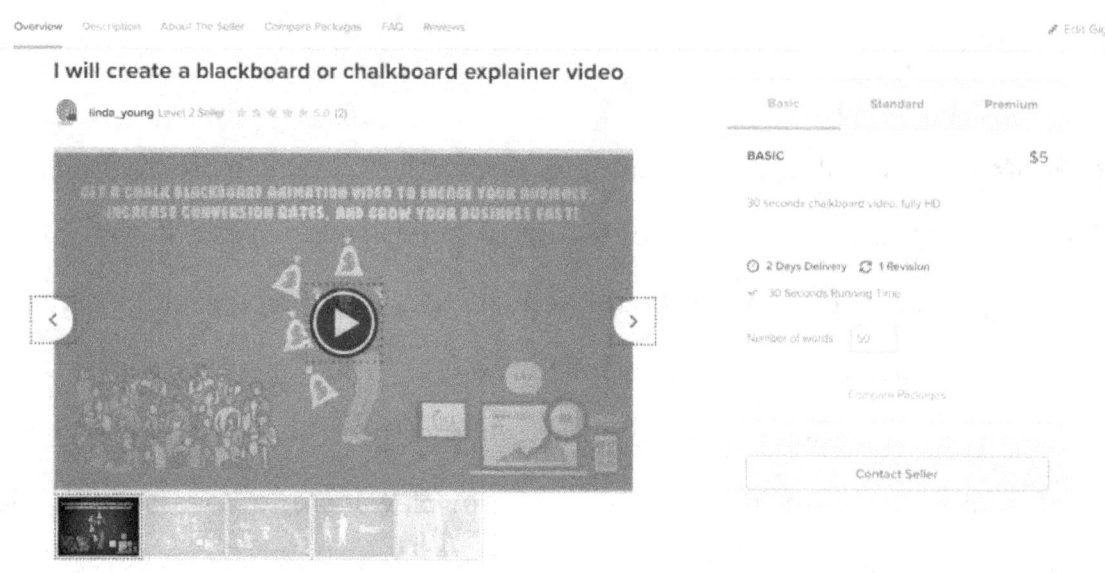

This is the final step towards creating your gig. Simply click the "Publish Gig" button and it'll go live. Once live, your gig can then be promoted through a social platform, such as Facebook or Twitter, simply by clicking the provided link. According to Fiverr, gigs that are promoted through social platforms are up to three times as likely to sell, so it's a good idea to consider this option.

In the next lesson we will cover the various levels of Fiverr as well as competitor analysis. I will share my personal experience of how I crossed these levels and how you too can do it.

Chapter 5

Fiverr levels, metrics and competitor analysis

Fiverr levels and their importance

I've said it before and I'll say it again.

Making decent money on Fiverr doesn't happen overnight. If your goal is to become a Top Rated Seller, you need to be handpicked by the Fiverr team, which will require a lot of consistency for a long time before that happens. However, even as a level 2 seller you can make decent money and in this lesson we will cover all the different levels of Fiverr, their importance and how you can climb those levels to eventually become a level 2 or top rated seller.

Figuring out how to make money on Fiverr is a long-term strategy, which will become more apparent after walking through details around leveling up as a seller and other considerations for keeping clients happy on the platform.

Let's break down what it means to sell on Fiverr at each level:

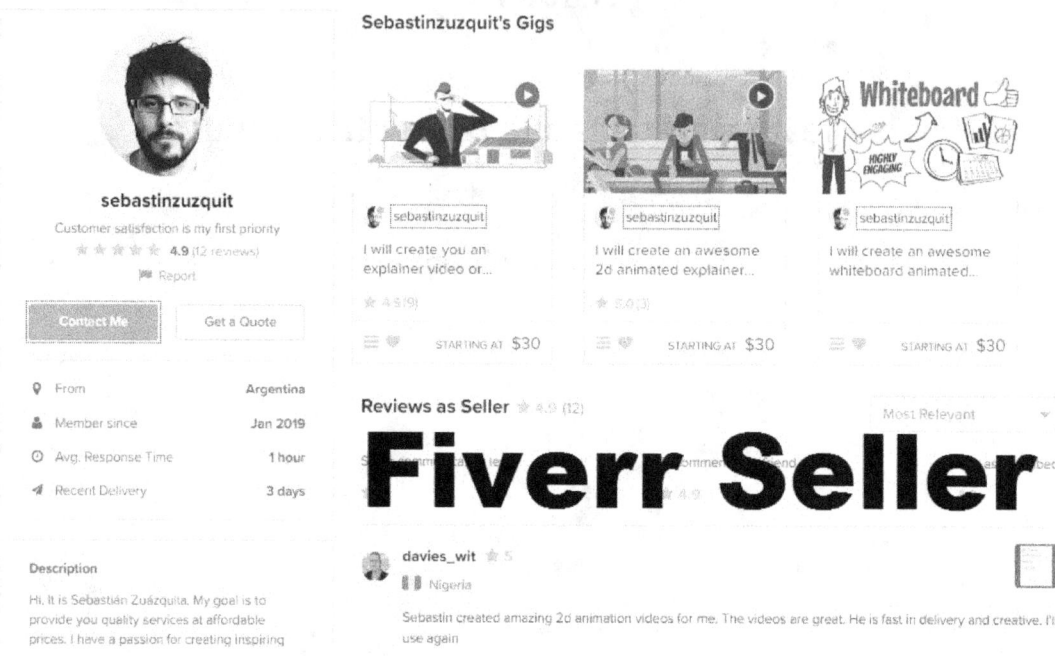

When you first sign up for a Fiverr account, this will be your level. Once you join Fiverr and create a Gig, you are automatically labeled as a New Seller. As a New Seller you will be able to enjoy the following benefits:

You can create 7 active Gigs

You can offer 2 Gig extras which are additional services you offer over and above your gig for an additional price as defined by you

5 Gig Multiples which means a buyer can place 5 orders of the same gig at one time

Send Customized Offers up to $5,000 to your buyers

Your payment will be cleared by Fiverr after 14 days

Fiverr's generic advice is to "work hard and play fair", which is not a bad generalization; although practically this is a toughest level to move up to be a Level One Seller. Moving up levels is beneficial because you'll receive more visibility in search, plus eligibility to be featured in promotional listings, like what happened to me when I became a Level One and then a Level Two seller. Leveling up also unlocks additional customization options around your gigs.

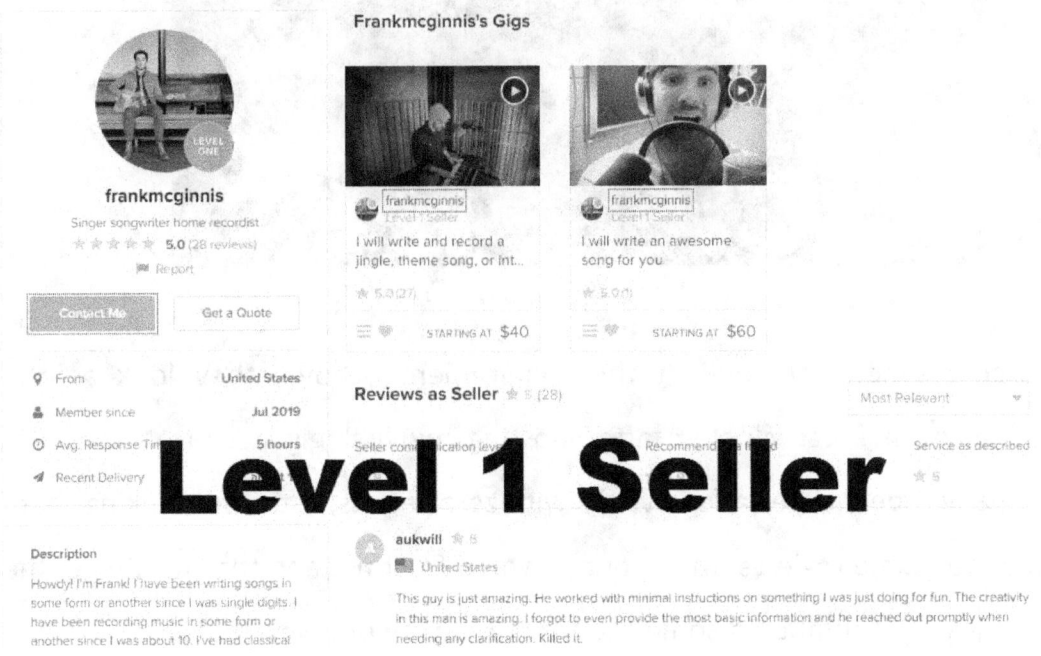

To reach Level One status, you need to fulfill the following requirements:

Complete at least 60 days as an active seller on Fiverr

Complete at least 10 individual orders (all time)

Earn at least $400

Maintain a 4.8 star rating over the course of 60 days

90% response rate over the course of 60 days

90% order completion over the course of 60 days

90% on-time delivery over the course of 60 days

Avoiding receiving warnings over the course of 30 days

Fun right? When you look at the requirements above, they look a little daunting; even I was clueless after posting my first gig because I was not getting any orders. After a few weeks with zero results, I started thinking that I need to get some reviews, then people would trust me and that would get me some sales. So, I contacted some friends to help me out with that.

I began promoting my Fiverr gig and started asking friends and family to avail my services and place a few orders. In other words I was also promoting Fiverr as a platform and now some of my friends have become regular users of Fiverr. These first few reviews from my friends were very critical for me. I think it took me around 8 reviews until I started getting real buyers. At first there were only one or two buyers a week and after that, slowly and steadily the flow of orders increased and I started getting regular orders and that's when my confidence grew with Fiverr. So I created around 7 separate gigs (which my basic seller level could allow) and continue to promote them among my immediate social circle while at the same time handling real buyers from Fiverr. Somewhere around that time I got the Fiverr level 1 seller badge, which allows you to have gig extras to earn more per order. These are the benefits of being a Level One seller:

10 Active Gigs

4 Gig Extras

10 Gig Multiples

Send Custom Offers, up to $5,000

Earning clearance: 14 days

Eligibility to be featured at promotional listings

My journey from being a Level One seller to becoming a level two seller was not that hard. By this time I was running 10 active gigs (as a level one seller) and had developed a loyal customer base that kept getting back to me for repeated orders. To become a level two seller, I had to fulfill the following requirements:

Complete at least 120 days as an active Seller on Fiverr

Complete at least 50 individual orders (all time)

Earn at least $2,000

Maintain a 4.7 star rating over the course of 60 days

90% Response rate over the course of 60 days

90% Order completion over the course of 60 days

90% On-time Delivery over the course of 60 days

Avoiding receiving warnings over the course of 30 days

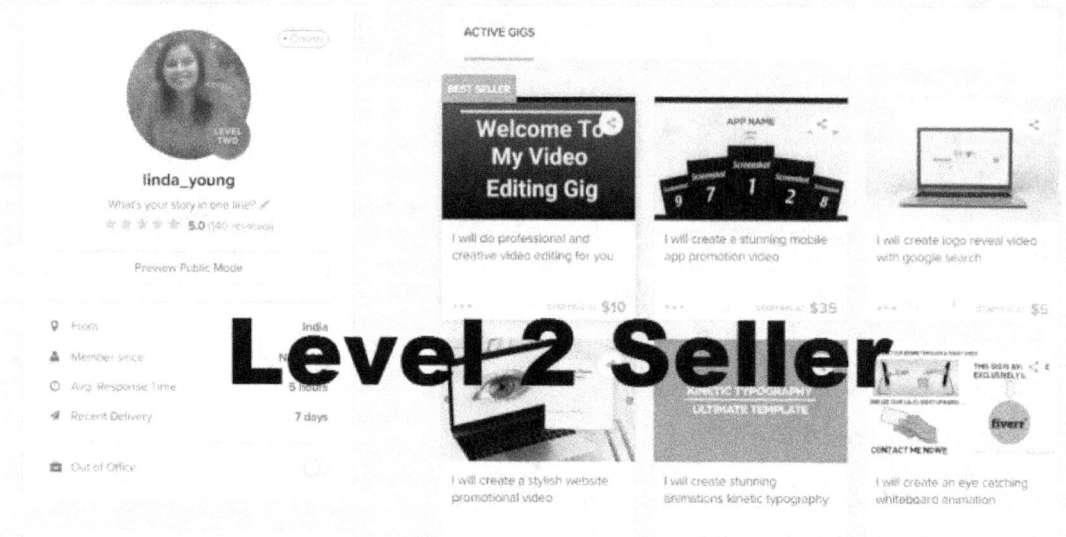

Aside from becoming a Top Rated Seller, Level Two Seller is the highest Fiverr level you can achieve on your own, automatically, by fulfilling all the requirements mentioned above. However, these requirements will be not difficult to achieve because as a level one seller you would have already gained the experience and understanding on how to deal with clients and get orders. If you are faithful to your work and this platform, it will only be a matter of time before you achieve level 2 status. As a level 2 seller, you will enjoy the following benefits:

20 Active Gigs

5 Gig Extras

15 Gig Multiples

Send Custom Offers, up to $10,000

Priority Customer Support

Eligibility to be featured at promotional listings

Eligibility for Customer Success program

Earning clearance: 14 days

One of the "benefits" of becoming a Level Two Seller is Priority Customer Support, however in my own personal opinion; I feel Fiverr mostly sides with the buyer. We will take more on this subject later. As a level 2 seller, you will be comfortably placed on Fiverr with regular orders coming from as many as 20 active gigs, should you choose to expand.

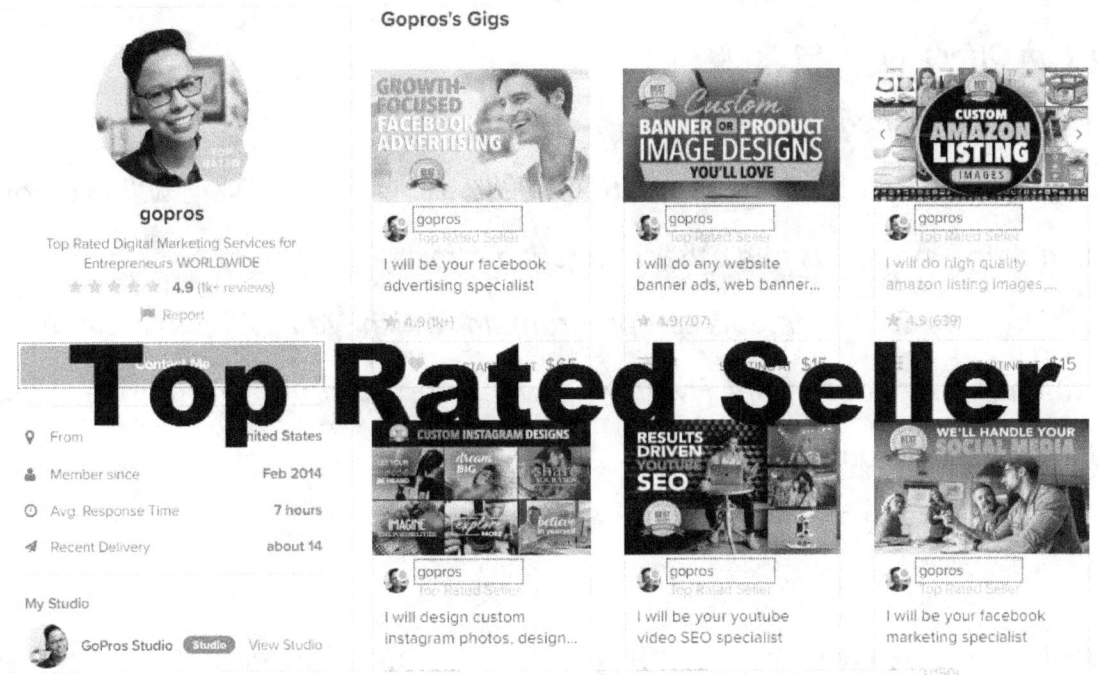

This is the highest Fiverr Seller level and I can assure you that it's not easy to achieve.

The process to level up as a Top Rated Seller is not automatic. You will need to be manually approved and in addition to your current metrics, Fiverr will take past performance into consideration. Notably, to qualify as a Top Rated Seller, you'll need to be active on Fiverr for 180 days, complete 100 orders, and earn at least $20,000 (in addition to maintaining good metrics more generally).

To put this into perspective for someone just starting out, it will take quite some time before you earn your first $20000. As a top rated seller, you will enjoy the following benefits:

30 Active Gigs

6 Gig Extras

20 Gig Multiples

Custom Offers, up to $10,000

VIP Customer Support

Eligibility to be featured at promotional listings (in which Fiverr will promote you in their emails, ads and other marketing efforts)

Eligibility for Customer Success program in which you will be assigned a Relationship manager from Fiverr who will help you grow your business and optimize your account

Earning clearance: 7 days

Needless to say, Fiverr will choose you as a top rated seller only if you have achieved considerable success as a level 2 seller. Becoming a Top Rated Seller is a serious business which means that Fiverr will be your ONLY SOURCE of income because you will probably be engaged 24/7 with serious clients who will pay handsome money for your gigs. That is why the earning clearance is 7 days instead of the usual 14 days with other levels.

The importance of metrics for leveling up on Fiverr

Maintain these standards to remain a Level Two Seller

- **Response Rate**: Respond to 90% of the inquiries you received in the last 60 days — 100%
- **Order Completion Rate**: Complete 90% of your orders, over the course of 60 days — 100%
- **On-time Delivery**: Deliver 90% of your orders on time, over the course of 60 days — 100%
- **Rating**: Maintain a 4.7 star rating, over the course of 60 days — 5

Achieve these goals to be nominated for a Top Rated Seller

- **Selling Seniority**: Complete at least 180 day as a seller — 180 day
- **Orders**: Receive and complete at least 100 orders (all time) — 100
- **Earnings**: Earn at least $20,000 from completed orders (all time) — $4,197 / $20,000
- **Days Without Warnings**: Avoid receiving warnings for TOS violations over the course of 30 day — 30 day

Looking through the various requirements for moving up as a Fiverr seller, I am going to share the basic context for the level of service you're expected to provide to customers on this platform.

Specifically, to maintain your level (without a downgrade) or move to the next, Fiverr expects you to maintain:

A minimum average 4.7 star rating

90% response rate over 60 days

90% order completion rate over 60 days

90% on-time delivery over 60 days

No warnings over 30 days

This is easier said than done especially because some aspects of these metrics are completely out of your control. Let me give you an example:

ORDER DISPUTE

stated the issue is:
This I ordered by mistake, thought seller will do animation video, script and voice over. But not

 Hi, As the seller is expert only in Whiteboard video, we need an expert who can do scriptwriting, voice-over and whiteboard, video maker.

would like to cancel this order.
You need to respond within the next 2 days,
or the order will be automatically canceled.

You Responded To Rahulreynolds's Dispute

09:50 August 13, 2019

ORDER CANCELLED BY MUTUAL AGREEMENT
You accepted to mutually cancel the order with

The other day, someone bought one of my Gigs to create a Whiteboard animation and then asked to cancel it because he could not provide the script or voice over and he expected me to render these additional services. I agreed to his consent and the order was cancelled. After that, I contacted Fiverr support to know if my order completion rate would be affected because clearly I was not at fault and this is what they had to say:

Hi Linda,

Please keep in mind our cancellation statics are handled automatically, and the system will update the cancelation rate based on the cancelation criteria, we recommend you check your analytics section to confirm. Before you do, please clear your browser's cache and cookies.

Fun, right?

The fact that Fiverr can't manually change aspects of the seller level algorithm in situations such as this is enough to make your blood boil.

But, all of this is to say that you can't control everything, especially when you're building your freelance business on somebody else's platform. You'd better come to terms with that now if you don't want to be driven insane on Fiverr.

Here are a few tips for avoiding bad metrics in general:

You automatically get a 1 star review if you're late to deliver and someone cancels the order. So basically, avoid delivering late at all costs since this can also affect your on-time delivery metric. If necessary, you can opt to extend the order with approval from your buyer.

Over delivering on expectations is a great way to guarantee 5 star reviews, which is an important metric for leveling up or maintaining a seller level. For instant you have a content writing Gig, this might mean going slightly over word count. If you have a UX audit Gig, this might mean filming a few extra minutes on a screen recording. And over delivering doesn't mean sacrificing profits, you will be pleasantly surprised that a happy Fiverr customer can leave you a good tip. This has happened with me on many occasions.

.

Keep your response rate in the green by replying to all new messages within 24 hours. Even if you need time to think of a good response, respond ASAP to set expectations for when you'll get back to someone. I'd recommend setting a calendar reminder to do this at the same time every day, so you don't accidentally fall behind. Though response time isn't a metric that affects your levels, it might be a factor when people are deliberating between working with you and another seller. It may also be a factor in Fiverr's search algorithm for recommending Gigs to buyers.

Use "Out of Office" mode to pause new orders and even incoming messages if you need a break. If you're serious about making money on Fiverr, you'll realize that it's better to lose out on some orders than compromise your metrics.

As to what the future of metrics might look like? This is what Fiverr PR Manager Holly Steffy has to say. *"Order completion, star ratings, and on-time delivery have always been among the top metrics"*. She adds, *"As the platform has grown, we are always looking out for what metrics are the most important for our buyer community and reflect that in how we measure a seller by their success"*.

Now that you understand the differences between each Fiverr level and how to level up from one to another, it's time to address a harsh truth.

On Fiverr the customer is always right even when they're completely wrong

This is really my main gripe with Fiverr. By nature of completing so many orders and being on the platform for so many years, I have dealt with a few bad eggs. No matter the situation, in most cases, when a buyer decides that they don't like your work, they will get a refund and it will come out of your earnings.

It doesn't matter what "proof" you share with Customer Support; there have only been a handful of situations where I've come out on top with disputes. So I'm warning you now that if you invest your time in Fiverr, there will be some frustrating situations ahead of you. That said, these situations will become fewer and farther once you have spent sufficient time and get a handle on how to deal with clients.

Here's a good example of the frustrating divide between how Fiverr treats buyers compared to sellers:

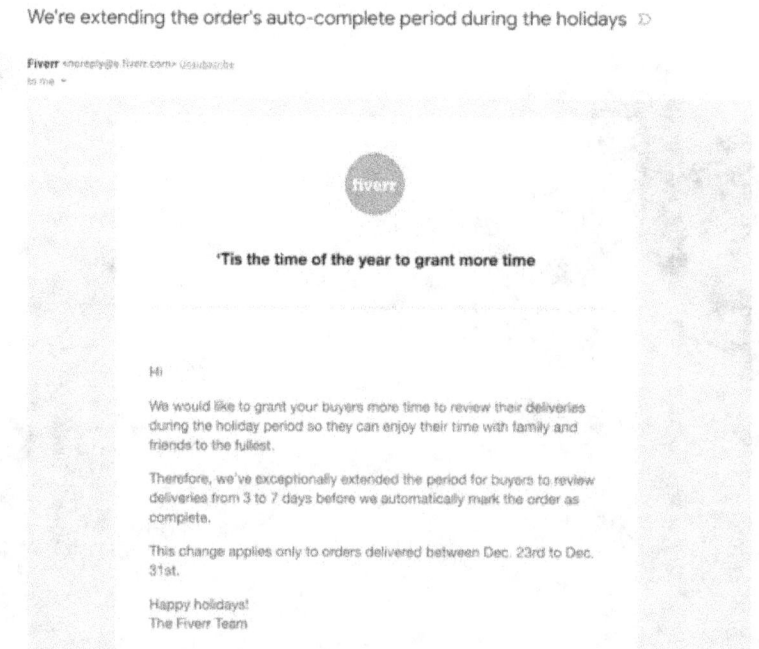

In this situation, Fiverr chooses the buyer over the seller in the following way.

Because buyers have an extended review period, orders completed on time will be paid out to the seller three to seven days later than expected. The seller is not given any additional business days to complete an order during the holidays, making it feel like their time is worth less than the buyer.

In general, the cheaper your prices on Fiverr, the worse the class of buyers you'll be dealing with. And this is just as true outside of Fiverr: the cheapest clients are usually those that expect the most from you while being the most difficult to work with.

It's worth noting that if you start your business on with cheap prices, it will be hard to later increase pricing with the clients you've already worked with and who keep coming back to you for repeated orders. So ideally, start with sustainable pricing and adjust as necessary when you gain more experience and knowledge.

The real key to limiting awful client interactions on Fiverr is to be crystal clear about the nature of the deliverable you're providing with each Gig package. You must also do your due diligence when collecting information from the client with the set of questions (known as Gig requirements).

Finally, set a limit for revisions (ideally, not more than 3), so that you and the client are on the same page about what's included.

My standard offering for my gigs includes just two to three revisions. This has helped me to get good reviews, earn great tips, and retain loyal customers. But if you want to successfully make money out of your gigs, do whatever you can to give people what they want the first time, otherwise, revisions can take so much time that your Gigs are no longer profitable.

Research Competition to see who is selling what

So welcome to this lecture where we will take a look at how top rated sellers have designed their gigs.

OK so the first step in finding the perfect gig for you is really to do some market research. So I suggest you spend about 20 or 30 minutes going through the top selling gigs on Fiverr and you're going to start looking through the 150 or so categories that are listed on the Fiver's site here.

Pay attention to the sellers with hundreds or thousands of reviews, and a star rating of 4.7 or higher. That's who you want to beat. As you browse their profiles, look for:

1.) How they describe their service

2.) Whether they're offering something you can also offer

3.) If there are any extras you can offer that they don't offer

4.) Scroll down to the end of their gig description, and check out the keywords they use to describe their gig. Make a note of these for when you create your own gig.

Research this for multiple sellers till you feel you've got a handle on what buyers in your niche really want? You need to figure for yourself that which gigs are interesting to you and how you can use that information to create or improvise your own gigs for your buyers. So let's get started.

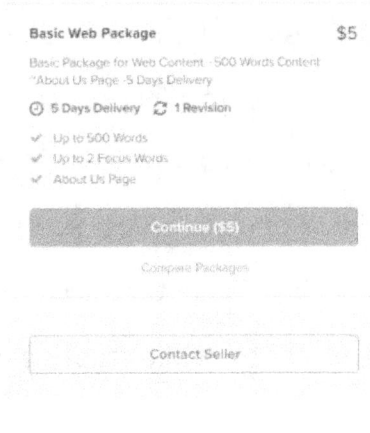

So as you can see over here, this gig falls under the category of "writing and translation' and it mentioned here that "I will write an About Us page for your web site". Now this is something that you can easily do if you have knowledge of Basic English. Let us look at this gig in detail.

So the delivery period here is five days. She must be getting a lot of work that is why she has a longer delivery period. In my case, I would reduce it to 3 days.

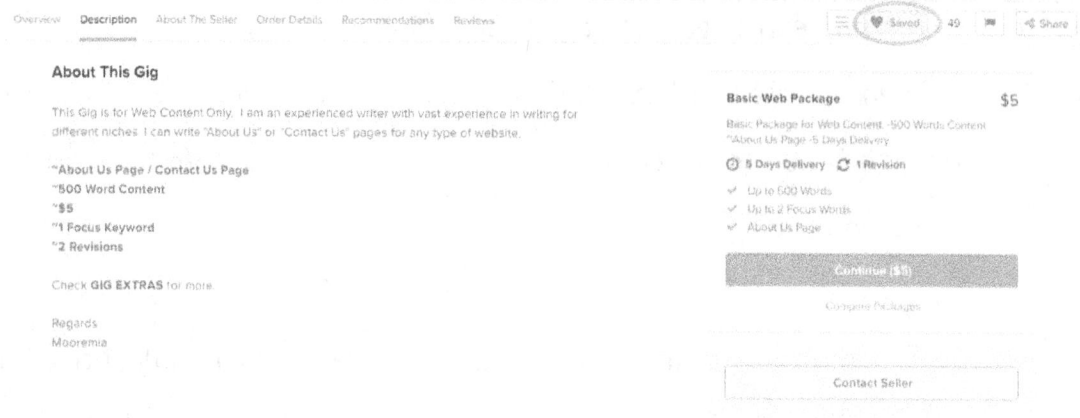

I will also add a URL in the description to maybe show samples of my work. I will definitely change the pricing structure and structure it into 3 packages so that the customer gets more options. So whenever you take a look at a successful gig, you should evaluate and figure out how to take the best points out of it and incorporate the same while creating your own gig. I will also "save" this gig so that I can come back to it whenever I am creating a new gig for a similar service in the near future. Like this I will take a look at 10 to 15 gigs and "save them" so that I can come back to them and select the best ones to refer to, while creating my own gigs.

Let us take a look at another category with a different skill set. Here's one.

Intros and Outros

So a lot of people use an intro before their main video in YouTube and social media ads. You can create a very basic intro and sell it successfully on Fiverr. It may require some technical skill but there are lots of free videos on YouTube which teach you how to make intros fairly quickly and easily. Just to give you a sense of what an intro video actually is let uslook at this gig.

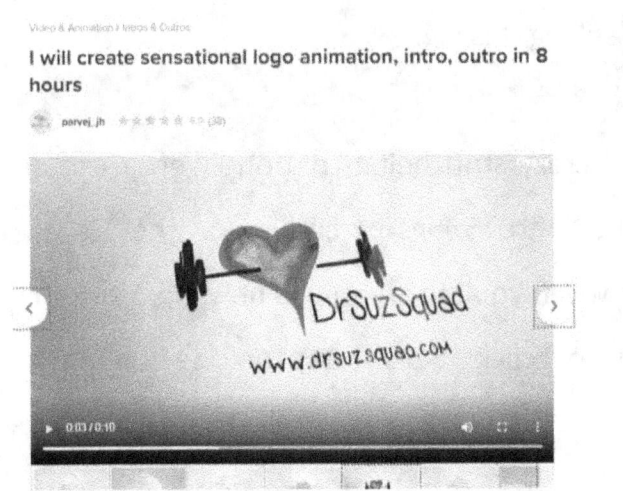 

So in this intro video you see the logo of the company as well as the tagline. That's all there is to it. A little bit of animation and you to need to simply add the logo and tagline. I am myself running three gigs on intro videos (although they are more advanced in animation). However, as I mentioned earlier, you can even create simple intro video gigs and they will sell well on Fiverr if it is appealing to the buyer. I am going to favorite this gig so that I can refer to it later. Let us have a look at another interesting gig. Here is a unique one.

 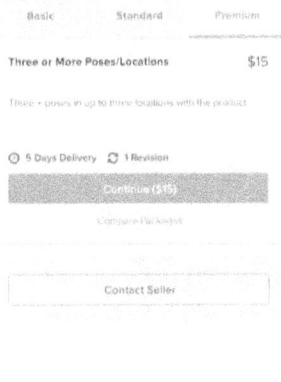

So this guy is selling a gig in which his pet dog models for pet products such as toys, treats, leashes, or clothes. What a great idea. He has already reached level 1 status with only 27 reviews. I had to work twice as hard. The dog is so cute; it is already doing a good job in selling this gig.

As you can see, there are all sorts of crazy stuff being sold on Fiverr. Take a good look around Fiverr and earmark 10 to 15 gigs by clicking on the "Save" butting so that you can refer to them when you are creating a new gig. You can view all your earmarked gigs when you click "Saved" tap on the top right section.

Competitor analysis does not mean copying somebody else's gig. Do not make the mistake of copying anybody else's gig because Fiverr algorithms are quite strong and you will not get a favorable search impression if your gig is copied. The idea is to study your competitor's gig and then come up with ways in which you can make your gig unique and attractive.

Chapter 6

How Fiverr is better than other freelancing platforms!

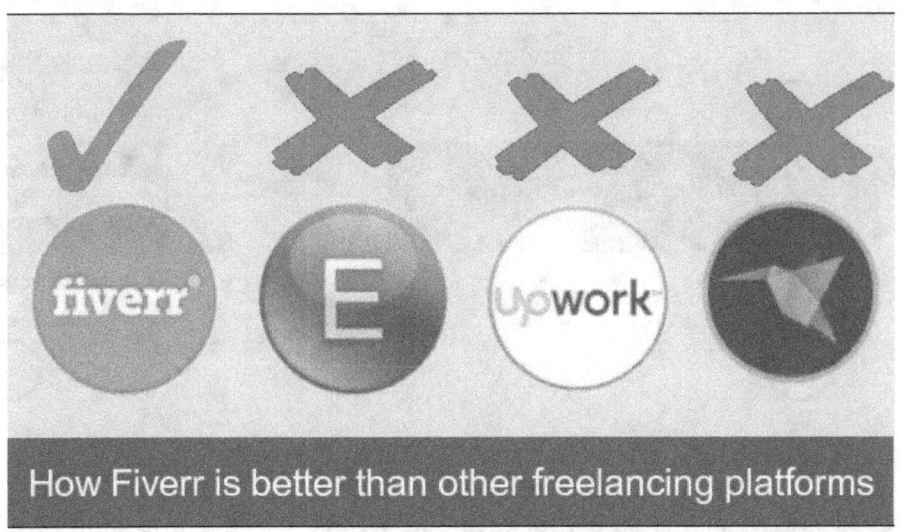

Alright, if you want to be successful on Fiverr, the first things you need to understand are the type of buyers who visit Fiverr. Who are these buyers? Why they are here and how is Fiverr different from the freelancing platforms out there? The reason it's so important to understand this is because you want to optimize and leverage your services in a way that differentiate you from other competitors on Fiverr. That is what will make your gig stand out and obviously Fiverr is going to promote you and feature your gigs if you do those things. These things that I am telling you are based upon my own experience that I've picked up over the years. So please make a proper note on what I am about to say because it's important to understand that this will make a huge impact to your success on this platform.

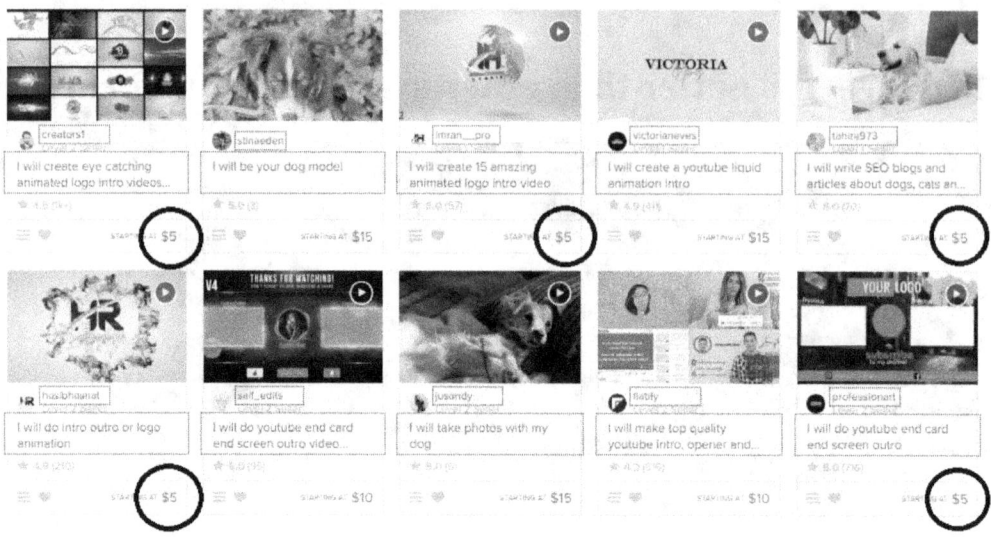

So as we all know, Fiverr is a marketplace where buyers and sellers come to trade. Buyers have an option to purchase services from over 150 categories of services across Fiverr homepage like for example logo design, article writing, and video editing and so on. However, the main reason why buyers come here is because of the price point. You can see that most of the services on Fiverr start at five dollars. Essentially buyers come here looking for a bargain. They come here to get value for money. As a seller you've got to realize that's the kind of a mindset of the person you're dealing with. They're looking for bargains and you've got to make sure that you're the one to deliver it.

So what types of people go for a low price point? My take is that roughly 60 percent of the buyers are small online or local businesses. They are here because they do not want to hire permanent employees for their lack of technical skills. They would rather outsource tasks to skilled people for a competitive rate on job to job basis. The second category of people is freelancers like you and me. They know how to game the system. Typically, what they do is offer additional services to their permanent clients and they buy these services from someone at Fiverr at a lower price to sell it to their client at a higher price. My guesstimate is that they would be about 20%. 10% of the customers are actually serious clients from multinational companies. Over the years, Fiverr has been targeting top end clients and they have started buying services from "Top Rated" or "Pro Sellers" on Fiverr. The last 10% are people who essentially buy non-business services on Fiverr. There are a lot of non-business gigs that sellers have created just for fun such as celebrity impersonations or reiki for pets and animals. You will be surprise to know that these kind unique services sell like hot cakes and there is a substantial market for it out there.

So those were the main points I wanted to make. Who are those buyers and why they are here? Four categories of buyers and that price point is the main thing that drives the buyers.

Now let us take a look at the differentiators for the platform itself. Fiverr is designed like a social marketplace. You can see that there's a big section for video and clear profiles of the sellers. You can also note the detailed statistics about their engagement and responsiveness. Go through all the reviews of the sellers before deciding on buying their services. Therefore, you've got to be a social person yourself as well. You've got to engage people with your profile by adding pictures and videos. You will get more success by projecting yourself as a real person. As with any other business, it's a lot about customer service and having a face really helps improve trust and that really helps in a marketplace where prices are low and that's how the platform compensates.

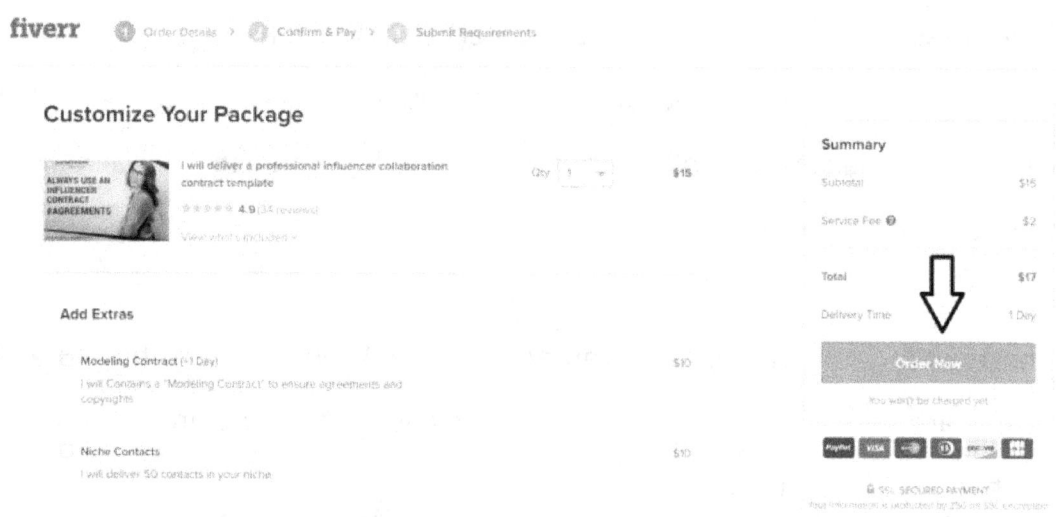

The other key difference about this freelancing platform is that it's kind of like a "click and buy" service. Fiverr is a place where you can purchase any digital service in just one click. This is a place where you can buy or sell services and avoid negotiating. You don't have to look for customers. People will come and avail your services. So what does that mean for you as a seller?

Well, you will want to develop a gig that is automated in such a way that the buyer can place an order without having the need to contact you. The buyer has the option to buy the same thing over and over again and this is great in terms of scaling because you are providing a service that you can repeatedly fulfill. That's very different from normal freelancing sites. For example, in

Elance you generally set up calls with customers where you pitch your price and there's a lot of back and forth negotiation there. The buyers have to find out what they need, discover all their needs; it's a much bigger process there. In Fiverr, the process is much simpler, the price is listed for a specific service and the buyer can choose to buy it without really talking to you.

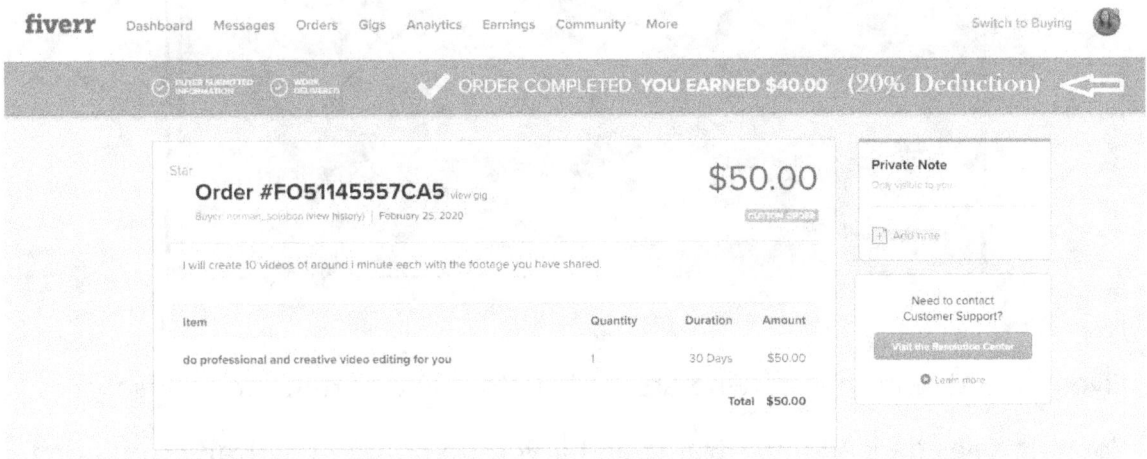

The final thing I want to talk about is the commission that Fiverr deducts on your price. Fiverr commission is 20% which means that on a $5 order, you will receive $4 as revenue and $1 will be deducted as commission. On the face of it, 20% commission seems quite high. However, if you look at it closely, this is actually a fair amount. Let me explain you why?

Fiverr delivers the customer right at your doorstep. If you have the right gig which appeals to the customer, you really do not have to do any marketing at all; Fiverr will do it for you. If you've ever tried to drive traffic online to get people to buy your service or product, you will know that not only is it difficult but it also costs a lot of money and time. If you are familiar with Google Adwords or Facebook Ads, you know how much it will cost to optimize and run these ads. You can avoid all that with Fiverr. If you can get a customer to your door for $1, you're doing pretty well for yourself.

Fiverr is flush with buyers who are looking to buy different types of services. Your gig sales depend upon traffic and if you do not get any traffic you don't make any sales. Fiverr makes money when you successfully deliver and complete an order. So you are not paying anything upfront, you make a sale, earn 80% revenue and pay Fiverr 20% commission, once the order is completed.

Please note that Fiverr is maintaining this site, millions of gigs and loads of traffic on a commission based model. They have to take care of all of the technicalities like processing the payments, issuing refunds, resolving customer complaints etc. They have a great system in here for your gigs. For example, if a buyer is not happy with the delivery, he can ask for a revision or ask for modification. That order can also be cancelled with the mutual consent of a buyer and seller. Hence there's a whole process that is set keeping all these scenarios in mind. It also helps a lot with your own workflow because as a seller you are always on your toes because you have to complete your orders within a timeline. You need to work diligently to maintain your metrics as well. Maintaining a system that increases your efficiency levels is not easy. That is why I feel that the 20% commission which Fiverr is charging is totally justified.

So let us go through the main point covered in this lesson. There are four types of buyers that visit Fiverr, the small online and local businesses, freelancers themselves, multinational or top end clients and people who buy non-business services.

Remember that Fiverr is a social marketplace and you really want to be playing using those features and making sure you get a lot of positive reviews. Remember that you want to develop a gig that's highly repeatable and in terms of how you make money, you want to either go for big volumes or think about logging extras that can be added over and above the service.

In the nest lesson we will work on a few tips and strategies to increase your sales on Fiverr.

Chapter 7

Optimize your gig to increase sales and get a 4 figure income every month

Hello friends. In this section we are going to cover in detail, how you should set up or improvise your gigs to increase your existing sales by 10X and thus potentially converting your income threefold to set you on track for becoming a super star seller on Fiverr.

There are several techniques that you can apply to your gig to significantly improve your chances of earning more. With a few tweaks you can see your sales steadily improve, get repeat orders and ultimately work with buyers who have a clear idea of what you offer and are confident in ordering from you. Anyway, I know you want to get to the good stuff, so here we go ....

Step number 1: Add a video to your gig

One of the easiest ways that you can get more sales on Fiverr is to add a video to your gig. That's very easy to do. For instance, if you are providing blogging services, you can create your own video sitting in front of your laptop or phone, and personally describe to your potential clients, what service you are offering and what makes you different from other buyers so that they buy this gig from you. Likewise, you may also get a professional video created for your gig on Fiverr for as low as $10 and there are many freelancers who are offering these services at a competitive price. The maximum length of the video is 75 seconds, so pack in as much information as you can to capture the attention of your customer.

Even Fiverr says that having your own video is guaranteed to boost your sales. So it's absolutely huge and critical especially for new sellers who are looking to get early sales through Fiverr. Think from the point of view of the customer. Whenever they are looking to buy a service, they scroll through the options on the webpage and if a gig displays a human face, they are more likely to click on it. Even if you have created an attractive thumbnail to showcase your service, make sure to have a video uploaded on the gig.

So for example, let us take a look at the image above. The video occupies a huge portion of the page. It's right at the top of the page and so it's very likely that somebody is going to click on this once. The important thing over here is that if they see your face or at least hear your voice it builds a lot of trust and more trust makes it easier for people to part ways with their money. So that's a huge factor. Once you submit your video it won't go up automatically as it needs to be reviewed by somebody. Make sure that your video is strictly oriented to what you are offering in the gig and include the phrase "this gig is available exclusively on Fiverr". This way the Fiverr authorities will know that this video is exclusive for your gig and they will go ahead and clear it.

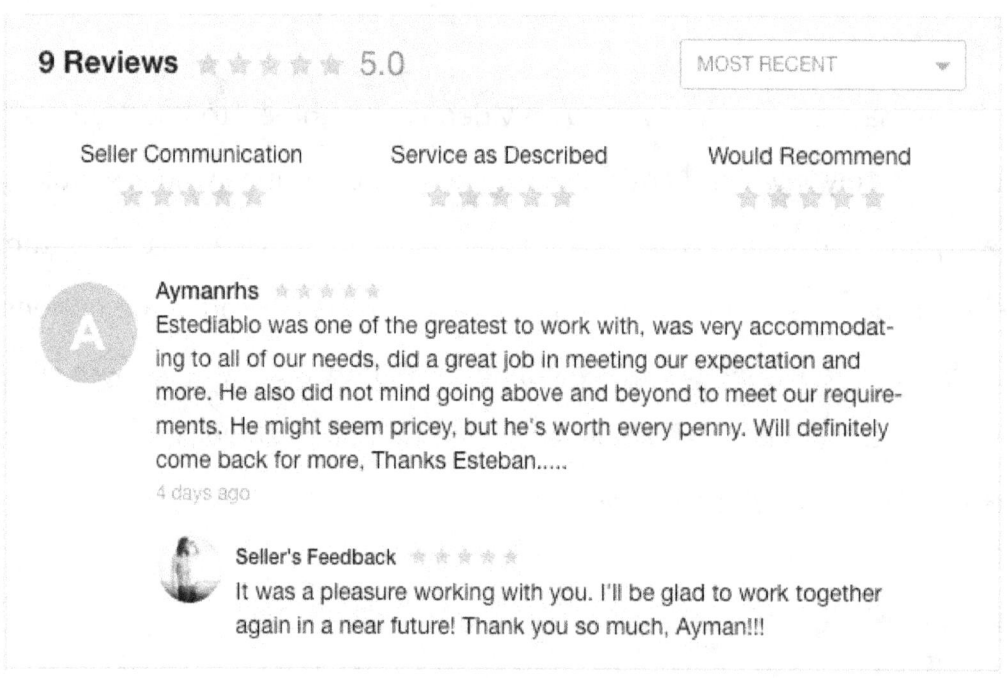

For existing sellers on Fiverr who have made some sales, it is always good to add screenshots of happy Fiverr clients in your video and especially screenshots of 5 star reviews and comments that buyers gave after availing your services. This showcases your credibility in the eyes of the customer and they are more likely to take a chance with you. For instance, there are others too who can write a blog. However your credibility is what that will differentiate you from other sellers.

The video can also be used as click bait for customers to read your gig thoroughly. In the video, always ask the customer to check out the description below to see the full details and the additional services that you are offering in the form of extras. Then finally you bring the "call to action" in your conversation by asking them to go ahead and click that order button. So you see, having a voice and a face is essential to build the initial trust with your customer. Having a video will help you stand out against the competition and it'll surely get you more sales.

Step Number 2: Optimize your gig title to get more number of clicks

So the next crucial step in your gig is to work on your title. You've got 80 characters to build your title and there are really two reasons why you want to spend some time to do this. Number one is that you want to include the key word of what you're offering so that Fiverr knows within its own search engine of people who type in services here, that they know what your gig is about and that it can be matched with the keyword or category of service that the customer is searching for.

So you know if you're offering the "logo design" you want to include "logo design" in your title. The other reason is that remember you're operating in a marketplace. Customers are going to compare these offers primarily by looking at the title and then the image or video that appears with it. So apart from your title being primarily a keyword to draw traffic, it also has to be catchy to draw the attention of the customer to choose you're from the rest of the gigs that appear in the search result of that page. The purpose of the title is to not only tell people what they are getting but also to get them to click on it; so you want something good that stands in the market place as well.

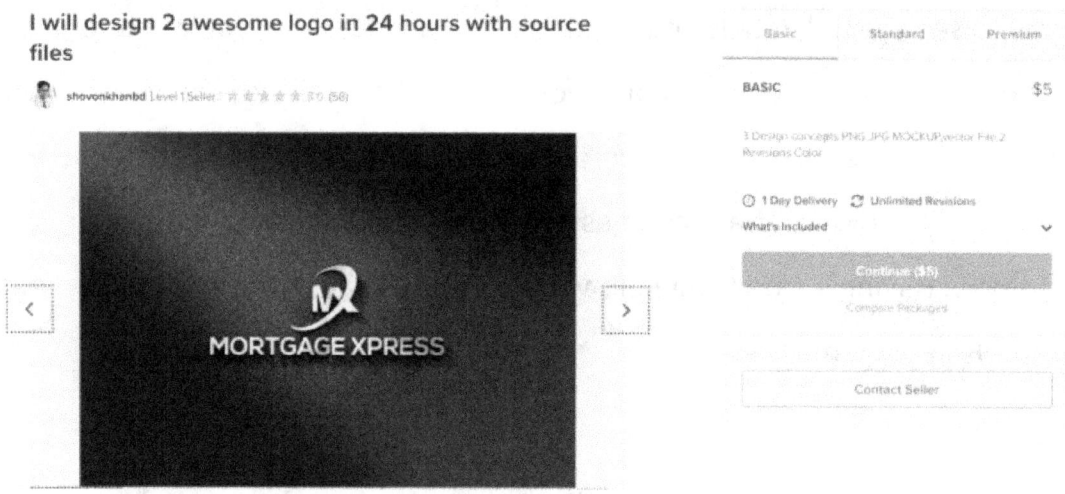

One thing that works well and what I recommend is that you focus on the result that your service will give them. So this gig here in the image above is a great example. The title says "I will design 2 awesome logos in 24 hours with source files". Getting two logo designs in 24 hours is a great offer and if the results are great with positive customer feedback, this gig will start appearing regularly in all search results driving lot more sales and traffic for you.

So take some time to work on gig's title. Think from your client's perspective as to what he is looking for and then come up with a title which is not only result oriented but it also has the appropriate keywords to regularly come up in search results.

Step number 3: Write a winning gig description

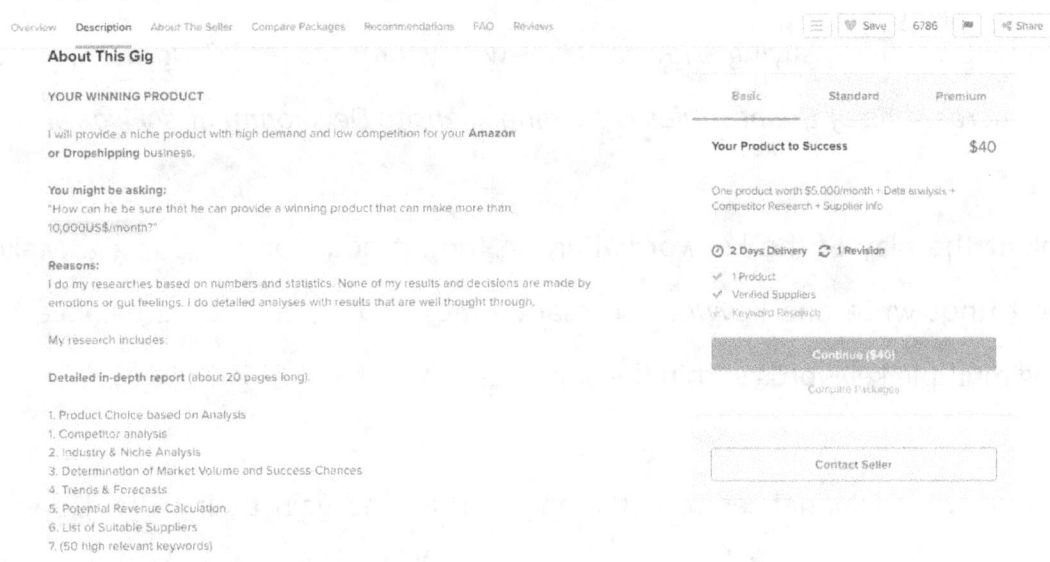

This is probably the most important feature of your gig and an area where you must show good creativity. This is quite a long lesson so I request you to please bear with me here. A great description for your gig will help get you a lot more sales. It's particularly important because this is the next thing the customer sees after your video or images. So far the title and the video/ images have drawn the customer to your gig. Now the description portion is the area which is your point of sale and the customer will take a final decision based on what he reads in your description.

Your description must be specific and detailed in covering the following points:

What is your gig delivering?
What exactly are the benefits?
Why do you have credibility to deliver this gig more than other people?

Let's say that you are setting up a gig on "website development". The first thing that you should do is to give very brief introduction about yourself and then follow it up by saying *"Having issues with your websites? Congrats! You've come across one of the best gigs regarding Website Development & Fixation."*

Look at the play of the keywords here in the introduction of your gig. Make sure to not write one keyword so many times and try to keep a balance by using multiple keywords within the sentence.

Mention your Experiences to get them familiar and gain their trust. Do you have any previous experiences with what you offer in this gig? Write it down! It is very important to at least mention all the Services you can provide in a single gig.

For example this is how you can jot down your experience briefly without it becoming a monologue.

"Below are some of the things I have previously worked with:
Divi Builder
WooCommerce
Fix WordPress Issues
Avada Theme
CSS and JS Fixes
BuddyPress

This way the buyer gets the idea of your skill sets and he will know how to proceed further with you.

List out the top core benefits of ordering your Gig, this can include:

What extra are you giving to the buyer?

How quick you are delivering?

How many satisfied buyers you have before?

What is the one thing you are offering that the buyer cannot find in other gigs?

Any other similar thing that comes to your mind

Every gig is different. Some gigs are clear cut in what they are selling, so there in interaction need and the buyer can place order directly without really communicating with the seller. However for a lot of other gigs, the order has to be customized to suit the buyer's requirement. The onus is on you to explain to the buyer whether they should order directly, and if they do then what package can they order? In most of my gigs I follow this route. However, I have three gigs in which I ask the buyers to contact me and explain their requirement so that I can give a custom offer. So even in your case, you need to explain to buyers that if their requirements aren't included in the gig then they should get a Custom Offer.

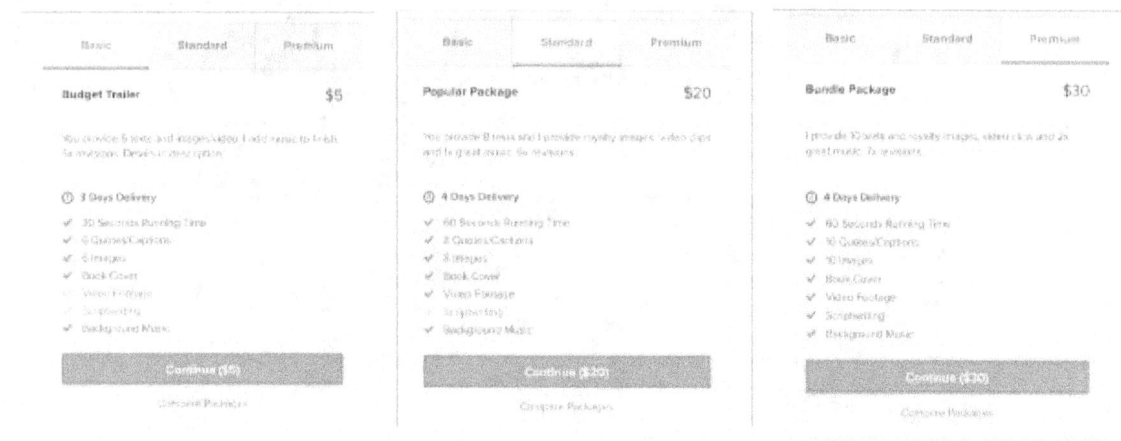

You can also explain in detail your gig packages and what extra benefit you customers will get if they go for higher priced packages. You can explain to the buyer, what you offer is in each package and what they should be expecting when they order from your Gig.

Make sure to use simple English, and not make it very confusing to read. Nobody has time to understand things that much especially on the internet. People have short attention spans. They are also quick and emotional when it comes to making a decision. The idea is to drive them to take action. To give you a sense of how a great description looks like, you take a look at this template below while creating gigs for your own services:

"Looking to get some outstanding [name your service]? Don't worry! I think you have found one of the best gigs regarding [name your service]. I have been working with [your service] for the last [years of experience] years which make me the right person to help you out with [your service].

Below is a list of things that I have experience with:

[a list containing all the tasks you have ever worked on related to the gig, you can keep these points bold.]

What you will get in this gig?

[Explain to the buyer the benefits of your gig]

If you need [some other service you offer] please see my other gig for that. Make sure to message me before ordering so we can discuss in detail and I can provide you a custom offer."

Note that the above gig description is hardly applying to all the categories. This template is just to give you an idea of how a well written description looks like. There is no point in copy pasting this template to use for your gigs because your gigs will then lose their uniqueness. Just make sure to use this template to showcase all the relevant things representing the services of your gig.

In the next chapter, we will cover a powerful feature of Fiverr i.e. Gig Extras. We will learn how to maximize the use of "Gig Extras" to increase the value of your gig substantially, thus driving more sales for you.

Chapter 8

Gig Extras: They will bring your real money in the long run

Gig extras are a fantastic way to increase the order value for your gigs on Fiverr and getting you to earn more from Fiverr. The gig extras may not be in your focus initially because you're more concerned with sales than focusing on increasing the order value. You want to make sure you get as many orders as possible and even if you're a level 1 seller your priority is to get though 50 individual orders to become a Level 2 seller.

By the time you are a level 2 seller; your sales volume will have increased. This is where you can shift your focus from order volume to order value. You need to start focusing on increasing order value and a great way to do that is to push people towards buying extras.

There are a lot of ways to push people towards buying extras. You can always limit your initial offer and add more value in your extras, thus prompting buyers to buy them. Like I said earlier, this thing will really work once you have achieved a certain status on Fiverr and a Level 2 Seller is a good point to start. So here's another example of a copywriting gig (I think I love these ha ha). The gig title is "I will solve all your copywriting needs". Given below is the description and pricing of the gig.

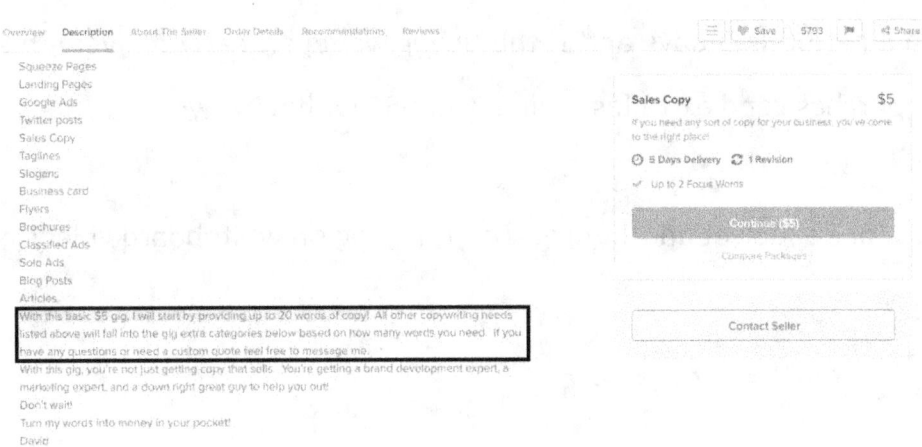

As we can see, the seller has done a very smart thing. Notice how the gig is priced at $5 for only 20 words. Now 20 words is essentially nothing, it will simply get you a headline for your topic. That leaves the buyer with no choice but to upgrade if he wants a copyright of 100 words. So let us take a look at the gig extras the seller is offering.

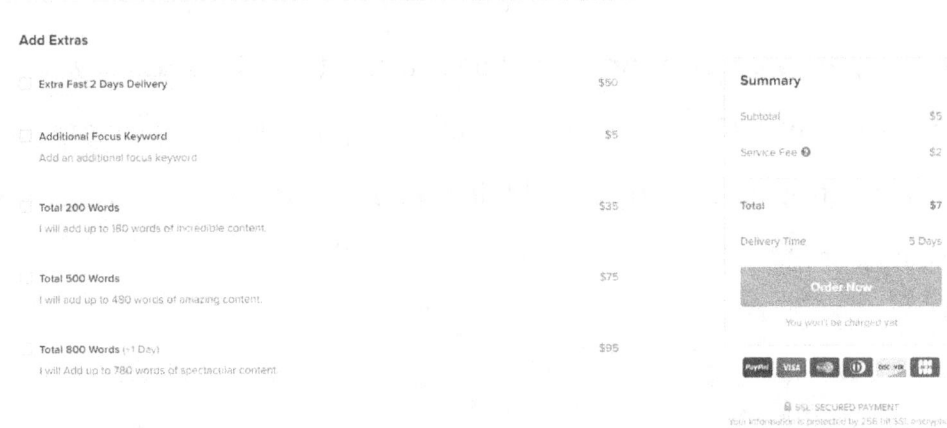

See how smartly he has priced his extras. There is one in which the seller offers 180 words for $35. So what happens here? The buyer ends up buying the gig extra and a $5 gig becomes a $40 deal for the seller. Not bad huh? At the very least, if the buyer does not want to pay $35 as extra, he can always message the seller with a counter offer to which the seller can respond with a customized offer mutually acceptable to both buyer and seller. Also not that the original period is 5 days and if the buyer wants an early delivery, he had option to purchase and extra fast delivery of $50 within 2 days.

Now let us take a look at another gig. This is my gig on whiteboard videos.

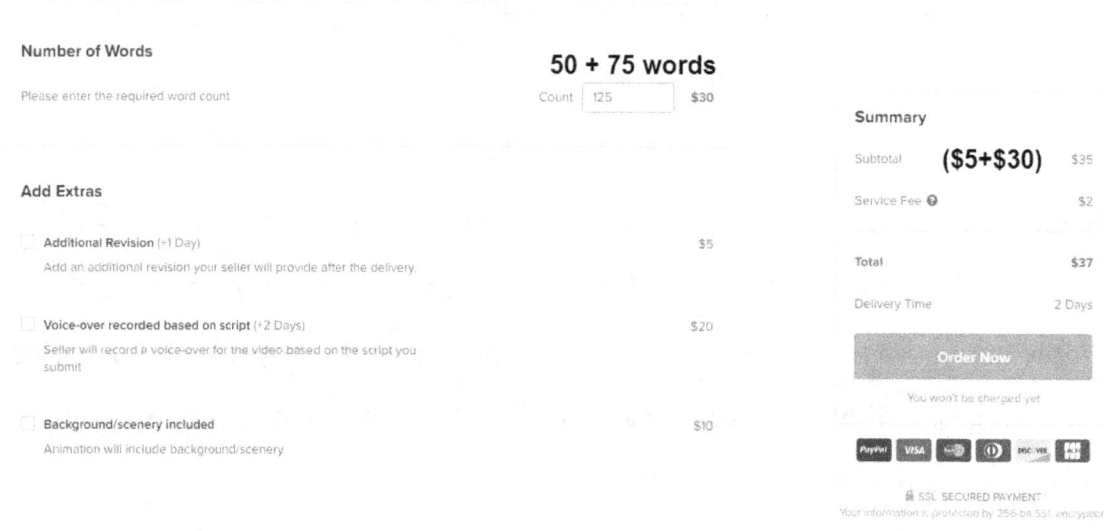

As you can see, the basic gig is priced at $5 for a script of 50 words. However, if the buyer's script has 125 words, he will end up paying $35 because I have priced my gig extras as $10 for an additional 25 words. Now what does the buyer do over here?

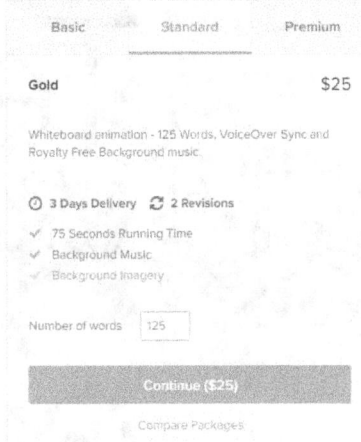

He will take a look at "My Standard Package" which is priced at $25 for the same number of words. So I was able to get the buyer to buy a higher package because I created a sentiment that the buyer is getting a good deal. These "extras' also play an important role in driving your buyer to opt for a higher package within your gig. As and when you start selling your gigs, you will need to figure out ideas to price your package in such a way that you can close orders at a higher value.

You can also add cheap gig extras that don't hurt the pocket so that the buyer can easily spend $5 or $10 to get extra value for your gig. For instance, in my subtitling gig I am offering the buyer the font color and background color of his choice for an extra $5. See. That doesn't hurt the buyer's pocket and its easy money for me. So again, take a look at your competitor's gigs and see how they have priced it especially the portion of "gig extras". Look at ways in which they have structured their gigs and derive inspiration from other similar categories or things that people are doing. You can also type your keywords in here to find gigs that may be in different categories just to see what are some of the gig extras that people might be offering?

Testing

In my experience, it takes time and a lot of testing to find out what works for you and what doesn't because every gig is unique. You need to structure your gig well so that people will actually upgrade.

There could be a scenario where you made your basic gig so limited that you start losing sales. In that case you will have to make your basic gig look better or make the gig extra an easy jump. Therefore there is no one way to do this. Like I said earlier, you have to look for inspiration from other people to see what's working for your particular gig and then it's going to take some testing and tweaking to really find the model that works best for you. Finally remember that this is something you should do only when you've become a level 2 seller and have good reviews under your belt.

Chapter 9

Unique Strategy: Drive more sales with a longer waiting period

Another way that you can make more money on Fiverr is to have a longer delivery period. The delivery time is very easy to change. It's under the pricing section in your gig and you can change it to as long or as short as you want it to be. You can go all the way up to 29 days. Now this might sound counter intuitive; if you deliver the gigs in a longer timeframe, people are going to be less happy. However, this is a neat strategy for you to get more sales.

I will advise you to apply this technique once your gig becomes more established and that you've got a good set of 5 star reviews on your timeline. When you are starting out, it is essential to have a quick delivery time because you want to build up those orders quickly. However, as and when you move up in the Fiverr levels, you need to capitalize on the business that you are getting, so once you've become a Level 2 seller, you can apply this technique to generate more revenue for yourself.

So how does a longer delivery period generate more sales for you?

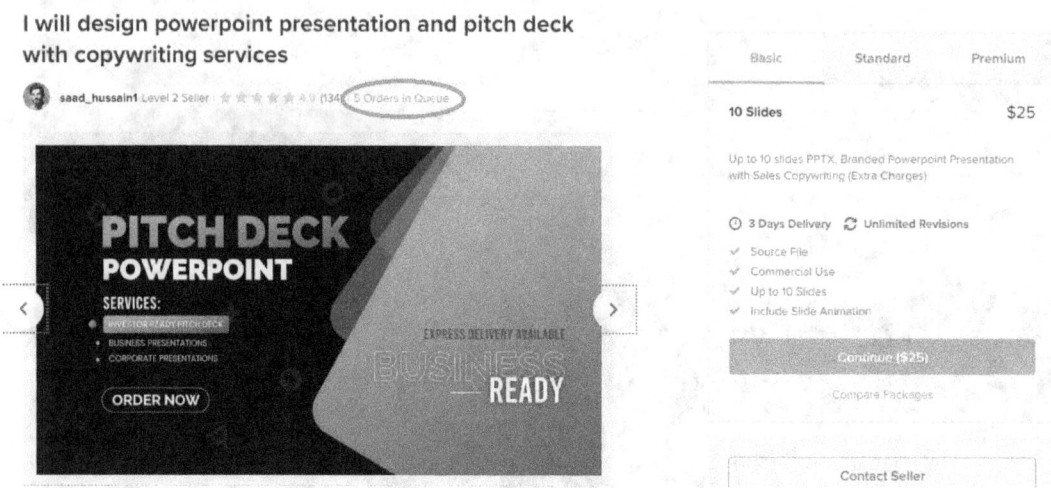

First of all, if you have a longer delivery time and you are delivering your orders slowly, you will notice that the fresh incomplete orders will start to queue up. So let us suppose, you have 5 orders in a queue, it will reflect on your gig page. The moment the buyers see that there are 5 orders pending on your timeline, it will give him confidence to immediately buy your gig. This is huge.

These orders are proof enough for the buyer about the quality of your gig and they're much more likely to get involved. I know that there are the reviews further down which they can see but this method creates a far better visual impact for buyers to turn their sentiment into a positive one for your gig.

Now the other way that it can make you more money is that you can gain "extra fast delivery". So if a person can't wait five days and if it's urgent enough for them, then they can pay extra to get the delivery in one or two days. As per my own personal opinion, people are comfortable paying anywhere between $10 to $20 (at the max) to get the gig delivered in one or two days.

The third and indirect way of making more money is to get the appreciation of the customer. Let us say that you have an order with a five day delivery and you deliver it in just three days. This shows that you've over delivered and you've given the customer something he wasn't expecting. This will again create a positive sentiment for your customer and he or she is more likely to leave you with higher ratings and review which in turn will drive more sales and improves your ranking.

So those are the three ways that a longer delivery time can make you money.

Number one is reflection of 'orders in queue" on your gig that will get people involved.

Number two is extra fast delivery.

Number three is that you actually deliver much before your stated delivery period which will create a positive sentiment for your customers and they're likely to give you a great review.

Hence I encourage you to use those strategies again maybe not initially when you set up your gig but definitely once you are established maybe as a Level 2 seller or as a top rated seller.

Chapter 10

How buyer reviews affect your sales on Fiverr

Words can lift someone's confidence and self-worth or break his spirit. That's particularly true of reviews that buyers leave for sellers on Fiverr. The online reviews are looked upon as personal recommendations from buyers and play a huge role in driving customer sentiment towards buying your gig. Fiverr metrics are quite demanding. You need to constantly maintain a 4.8 star to 5 star ratings on your profile otherwise you risk losing your level. Before we go for an in-depth study on buyer reviews, let me give you a quick knowhow of how Fiverr's level system works.

Fiverr level and rating system

I am currently a Level 2 seller on Fiverr. These are the minimum requirements I need to maintain to hold on to this level.

Maintain a 4.7 (94%) star rating over the course of 60 days

90% Response rate over the course of 60 days

90% Order completion over the course of 60 days

90% On-time Delivery over the course of 60 days

If you look at the above four points closely, you will notice that I need to maintain these minimum levels over a 60 day cycle or period. Fiverr does an evaluation of the metrics every 30 days on the 15th of every month. If for some reason, I am not able to maintain any one of these metrics over the course of 60 days, I will lose my status as a Level 2 seller and be downgraded to a Level One seller.

Alright, now please pay close attention because I am going to explain how these metrics are calculated on Fiverr. Let us say, that hypothetically there is a situation in which I was not able to deliver a couple of projects on time and my on-time delivery rate fell to 85%. On the evaluation day, let us say 15th January, these are my metrics.

Positive Rating: 5 stars

Response Rate: 100%

Order Completion: 100%

On-time delivery: 85%

As my on-time delivery is 85% which is below the minimum requirement of 90%, on 16th January I will lose my current Seller 2 level.

Now the next evaluation is on 15th February. I have a period of 30 days till 15th February to deliver more orders on time so that I can increase the "percentage of orders delivered" to above 90%. Let us say I am able to do that and the next evaluation on 15 February shows these statistics:

Positive Rating: 5 stars

Response Rate: 100%

Order Completion: 100%

On-time delivery: 95%

On 16th February I will again be promoted to a level 2 seller because I was somehow able to overcome the on-time delivery deficit and increase my percentage to 95% which is more than the minimum 90% requirement.

This is how the Fiverr metrics and level system works. You have to be extremely diligent in maintaining your stats to keep your existing level otherwise you will be demoted. Among the four metrics, buyer reviews can be significantly tough to maintain because they demand a minimum 94% rating to maintain your level. Let me explain how.

Let us suppose that over a course of 60 days, you were on a 15 day vacation and during that period you could only work on 10 orders. Now for nine orders you have done well and have received a 5 star rating. However, there was one order, in which you had fallout with a buyer and he left you a rating of 1 star. Now your overall stats reflect this:

9 orders x 5 stars = 45 stars

1 order x 1 star = 01 star

So you have received a total of 46 stars. If we divide it by 10 orders, your average star rating is 4.6. The minimum star rating you need to maintain is 4.7 but due to your rating being 4.6 you will lose your level. Just imagine. You did everything right to get 5 stars for 9 orders but just one order of 1 star ruined your stats and you had to lose your level. This has happened to a lot of buyers on Fiverr and even I have gone through this traumatic experience. Trust me, it is much easier to cover the deficit with the other 3 metrics but way tougher when it comes to buyer reviews because the minimum requirement is 94% and unless and until you have a steady flow of orders, it will take a lot of time before you cover this deficit.

Cancellations and negative feedback hurt in more ways than one. Not only do they affect your rating and sales, they can also affect your psyche. When someone cancels an order or leaves negative feedback, it can give you a feeling of confusion and frustration. This may lead to impulsive and bad actions such as messaging the buyer to demand a new review, or even worse, report them to customer service out of spite. Instead of taking a look at why you received the cancellation or bad review in the first place, actions such as these only compound the problem.

So this is one of the most important lessons you will cover in this course. We will look at ways and means to minimize your cancellations and poor reviews, if not eliminate them completely?

Fiverr review system for buyers and sellers

1 Reviews ★★★★★ 5.0		AUTO ▼
Seller Communication ★★★★★	Service as Described ★★★★★	Would Recommend ★★★★★

fiverr Fiverr-Social ★★★★★
Outstanding Experience!
9 days ago

Before delving deeper into the subject let us take a look at the following points to understand how the review system works for both buyers and sellers.

1.) The buyer has 10 days to leave reviews once the order is marked as complete.
2.) Once the buyer leaves a review, the seller will receive a notification and can leave his own review. Note: The seller cannot yet see the buyer's review at this stage.

3.) Once both the seller and buyer have completed their review or the 10 days have passed, both reviews will be made public.

4.) Reviews about the buyer will only appear in the buyer's profile.

5.) Once reviews have been made public, they cannot be changed.

6.) If the seller does not review a buyer within the 10-day period, he will not be able to add a new review for that order.

7.) If you feel that a review left by a user is abusive, a result of a technical error, or violates our Terms of Service, please contact our Customer Support team.

8.) After both seller and buyer leave a review on the order (or after 10 days), seller has the opportunity to respond to the buyer's review and explain his side in case of any misunderstanding. This will appear under the buyer's review in seller's Gig page.

9.) Seller can only respond once to the buyer's feedback. The response cannot be changed or edited unless it violates the values of Fiverr community.

Take a closer look at the 9 points above. You will notice that things are heavily loaded in favor of the buyer. Point number 2 says that once the buyer leaves a review, the seller cannot view it unless and until, he leaves a review first. This is a very tricky situation for the seller. The seller does not know whether the buyer has left him a favorable review so he will be confused whether he should favorably review the buyer or not. Let us suppose that the seller plays safe and rates the buyer as 5 stars only to find out that the buyer has given him a 3 star review. What does the seller do here? He cannot challenge the buyer because he has already given a 5 star rating to the buyer, thus making his case weak.

Now let us look at the opposite scenario. The seller is not sure whether the buyer is going to give him a favorable rating and based on his experience, he offers a 3.5 star rating to the buyer. Then it is revealed that the buyer has given him 5 stars. Now this becomes equally embarrassing for the seller. Not only has he given a low rating to a favorable buyer but he has probably lost this buyer's potential future business forever.

As you can see, both these scenarios create a dicey situation for the seller. However, over a period of time, you will figure out how to deal with this situation. Now that you have understood Fiverr metrics along with the review system, we will talk about the ways with which we can avoid negative reviews and get favorable ratings from buyer.

Six tried and tested ways to maintain minimum ratings and reviews on Fiverr

Let's be clear. Cancellations and bad reviews happen and it is not always the buyer's fault. There can be a project change, budgetary issue, time allocation or family emergency. Any of these factors can lead to you or the buyer cancelling. They can also lead to you not delivering what was promised or in fact not delivering at all, which is an automatic negative review. With that in mind, let's focus on five actions you can take to avoid bad reviews:

Let us remind ourselves of the basics that we have covered in our earlier lessons and that is to have a great Gig which covers everything that you offer in minute details and is easy for the buyer to understand. Having a clear title with a concise Gig description and selling packages should leave no doubt about what you are offering and for what price. Make your deadlines realistic so that you avoid delivering late which leave a negative impression with your buyer. Ensure your grammar is impeccable so to avoid any potential misunderstanding. Remember, the clearer you are with what you are offering, the less likely a chance for the buyer to order something that you does not offer out of confusion. And if they do, you can easily point them back to your clearly written Gig description and packages.

2.) Keep it Simple

When you communicate with a buyer about a particular project, keep things simple so that you avoid confusion. For example, you have a gig about writing a blog post and in your description you have mentioned things such as SEO optimization, link injection and competitor research and so on. All of this may sound great to you, but what does it really mean for the buyer? Most of the buyers lack technical sense and they can interpret these terms very differently. A buyer may think that SEO optimization is keyword research, which you are not offering. Therefore, instead of saying SEO optimization, you can say that you are framing bullet points and headings to help the content potentially show up in search results. This is simple and easy to understand. Likewise, you may choose to say that you place links in the content to point to resources that back up your research as opposed to link injection. By keeping the language simple, you avoid any confusion that can lead to a buyer wondering if they purchased what they thought they were supposed to get. This helps prevent a cancellation or a three-star review, which leads us to our next point.

3.) Never take jobs that you are not sure of Delivering

One thing that you should never do is to link or accept other jobs with your gig, especially if you do not have any experience of doing it. This is inherently a big risk because if the job goes bad, it will also affect the quality of the original job that was promised in your gig. Let me explain how.

You are a web designer so that means you are creative and great at designing. So if somebody gets a website designed and in addition also asks you to create a flyer for their business, you will be tempted to accept the job to make an additional $15, because after all, creative designing is your forte. However, you know nothing about the industry that the flyer is for and it would be unwise to accept this project as it is out of your realm of knowledge. If at all the buyer is not satisfied with the flyer, he may end up giving you 4 stars instead of 5 simply because the flyer did not work for him and thus he gave your 4 stars because he liked the work of your original gig.

Being a video editor I too keep getting additional offers to make a thumbnail or YouTube banner after I have created a video for them. My answer is a resounding NO. I am very clear and upfront with my clients that even though I can create a thumbnail, it will not be half as good as what some of the other sellers on Fiverr can do. If they are okay with a basic thumbnail, I can do it for free or at a minimal charge but this should not reflect upon the quality of my work. So communication is the key and I make sure that I let my clients know my limitation whenever an additional job is asked for over and above my gig offering. 99% of the times, the buyer will appreciate you for your honesty and will become your regular client.

Even while applying to buyer requests, you should avoid taking work which you are not sure of delivering 100%. This is especially important for new sellers who are just starting out on Fiverr. Applying to buyer requests that are not in your category or comfort zone is a risk which may lead to a negative rating. Over here the negative rating may be quite harsh because the buyer chose you out of several other offers and if you are not able to deliver or understand his needs, he will come down heavily on you. So take your time, it is much better to have a slow start on Fiverr then to risk getting a negative review right at the beginning of your Fiverr career.

4.) If you have doubts about the buyer and the project ....

Don't Take It !!!

I cannot express how many times I have read about this on Fiverr forums. A buyer contacts you with a potential project. Something seems off about the way the buyer explains the project, the nature of the project, or some other aspect. However, despite your better judgment, you go ahead with the project. When you begin working, you start to have some questions. You ask the buyer to clarify and you get a general response you think clarifies your concerns. You do the work and then deliver the Gig. Before you know it, you have either been asked to make multiple revisions or been told to redo the entire project. At this stage you have put in a lot of hard work and time and you want to avoid cancelling the Gig. You finally deliver what you think the buyer wanted, and he goes ahead and leaves a bad review. In this moment, you probably think to yourself if only you had trusted your instinct and not accepted the Gig; you would not be in this situation.

Therefore trust your instincts. If you feel that there is something off about the buyer and the project and you cannot place your finger on it, take that as a sign to not accept this order. I have gained a lot of perspective over my years of dealing with buyers so I always know when something is off while communicating with them. Hence I politely decline requests where I feel an iota of doubt about the project.

Like you and me, buyers too are human beings. They too like a little extra and that little extra goes a long way in creating a positive sentiment for the buyer. So a great way to earn positive buyer reviews is to keep the buyer expectation low for your gig while delivering extra, over and above the deliverables in your gig. Let me give you an example. If the buyer gave you an order to edit a document but did not order comments as a Gig extra, throw in a bonus comment or two. The buyer will not only be grateful, but who would cancel or leave a poor review on a delivery containing more than promised? If anything, you may get a review that says you delivered above and beyond, which is worth its weight in gold.

6.) Cancel the order to avoid a bad review

All said and done, despite being aware of everything and following the above five points to the tee, there still arrives a situation where the buyer is not happy with your work and wants to leave you a negative review. Under such circumstances, it is better to go for a mutual cancellation of the order then to get a negative review. In the beginning of this lesson we had discussed how difficult it was to recover a 5 star rating over the course of 60 days once you were reviewed negatively. However, for the other metrics it is not so difficult the requirement for order cancellation is 90% which can be made up before the next evaluation on 15th of each month.

Canceling the order is the only way at this stage to protect your reputation on Fiverr. If you have a relatively consistent flow of orders, you will easily make up the metrics to stay above the 90% requirement and after 60 days are over from the date of cancellation, you will jump back to 100%. However, don't make it a regular habit, because two cancellations over a short period of time will have the same effect as that of a negative review. Order cancellation should be the last option to exercise, when everything else has failed for you.

So these are the actions you can take to prevent negative reviews. Most of them have to do with having clear communication, setting expectations, and being honest. If you decide to do the right thing and follow the actions above you will not have to face such situations.

Avoid Asking Buyers for a Positive Review

This is a mistake most sellers tend to make while starting out on Fiverr. New sellers are desperate for positive reviews because they quickly want to climb levels to become a Level 1 seller. A lot of times, buyers do not leave any reviews despite accepting your delivery and marking the order as complete. Other times, buyer does not respond at all and the order is marked auto complete after three days and the money is credited to your account. Either way, as a seller, you may become baffled or confused as to why the buyer has not left a review? Out of desperation, you will start messaging the buyer to leave a positive review. DON'T DO THAT.

Not only is it wrong to solicit feedback from the buyer, it is against Fiverr's policies, terms and conditions. This is what they have to say.

"Do not manipulate buyers to provide positive feedback. It is against Fiverr's policies for sellers to solicit feedback from Buyers in exchange for refunds, discounts, upgrades or any other type of additional benefit."

This means that under no circumstances whatsoever you will ask the buyer to leave feedback for you. If you try to act smart and use vague language to solicit feedback, you will still violate policy and Fiverr takes very strict action in this regard. You may receive a warning from Fiverr for violating the rules, get an immediate suspension or a complete ban from the platform altogether. I have seen many sellers doing business for years getting banned from Fiverr for not following the rules. Over the last couple of years Fiverr has become increasingly strict in implementing their policies.

Just to put this in perspective, Fiverr on its own reminds the buyer 2 to 3 times to provide feedback on the order. Most of the times, buyers do leave a feedback but sometimes a buyer does not want to do so because he may not be really happy with your service. However, instead of giving you a negative rating, he has chosen not to leave a feedback at all. This in turn does not affect your ratings. So please understand this. If a buyer has not left a feedback, there is no point chasing him. He may not be happy with your service and it will become counterproductive for you to solicit his ratings.

Dealing with customer support for a rating you do not agree with

At some point you will face a situation in which you have received a negative rating you do not agree with or it could be a careless mistake of the buyer. Now as per Fiverr rules, once a rating has been given it cannot be changed. You are not even allowed to question the buyer as to why he provided the negative rating. All you can do is to respond to that rating with your own comments explain what you did right and what the buyer could not understand. All of this will be reflected on your gig's timeline.

This has happened to me also. A buyer ordered a gig from me and he was very happy with my service. He even left a $5 tip for me. However, when I saw the rating I was shocked to discover that he had given me 3.7 stars. I couldn't fathom what is happening and I quickly went through his feedback. There were 3 points on which I was to be rated. See screenshot below for reference.

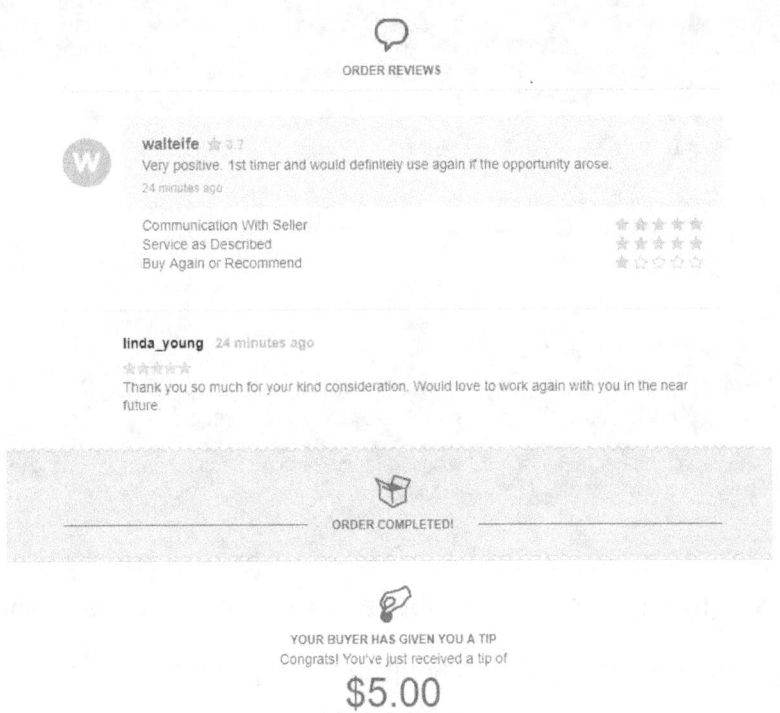

While I was given 5 stars for point numbers 1 and 2, he gave me 1 star for point number 3 i.e. "buy again or recommend". At the same time in his comments he mentioned that he will definitely use my services if the opportunity arose. So if the buyer wants to use my services again why will he give me a 1 star for "buy again or recommend". Just doesn't make sense right. So, despite my better judgment on violating Fiverr's rules, I went ahead and asked the buyer why he did that. As it turns out, it was a careless mistake on his part. He tried changing the review but he could not do it. At that time I was a Level 1 seller and I could not afford a negative rating. So I decided to contact customer support.

REQUEST #3112893
BUYER GAVE WRONG RATING BY MISTAKE

linda_young *December 01, 2016 00:26*

I completed an order against which the buyer was quite happy and he also left me a $5 tip. However, by mistake while rating me, he gave me 5 stars under two categories and 1 star under the 3rd category of "buy again and recommend". If you look at the the comments the buyer clearly says that he will hire my services again if an opportunity arises. As Fiverr takes its rating policy very seriously, we as sellers also take it very seriously and strive to put our best foot forward in providing these services to maintain a rating of over 4.8 stars. So any kind of mistake like this that affects our ratings on Fiver has a big impact on our business and performance. If an unfavorable review is genuine, then its okay but in case of mistakes like these, I urge you to kindly give us a chance to correct the mistake.
I have enclosed a screenshot for your review.

 Untitled.png (40 KB)

Hello Linda, *December 01, 2016 16:31*

Thanks for the information. I will need to review your request further to confirm. As soon as I'm able to provide you the details, I will follow up in this ticket request.

Please remember that it is against our Terms of Service to solicit feedback changes from buyers or guilt them into changing the review.

As you can see in the screenshot above, I explained my case thoroughly to Fiverr. They in turn responded by saying that they will review my request but it is against their Terms of Service if I solicit feedback changes from buyers or guilt them into changing the review. The first reply did not help and I took it in my stride that I will have to accept the review and carry on. However, to their credit, they took action fairly quickly and removed the review altogether.

These things can happen with you also. When you are in this situation, do not panic. Stay calm, assess the situation and if you think you have a case, make sure to compile a detailed response along with screenshots of the conversations between you and the buyer and present it to customer care. Be earnest when you are dealing with them. Chances are that they may side with you if your case is strong. If things don't go your way, don't lose heart, move on and focus on other orders.

Chapter 11

Five Methods to make your Fiverr business a roaring success

This is the most important chapter of this book. I will be discussing five methods that I applied in the last couple of years to seriously boost my business and bring myself to a situation where I might be earning more than a "Top Rated Seller" even though I am currently a Level 2 seller. One thing that I understood quite early was that I cannot depend upon Fiverr alone to get me clients. Your gigs may or may not invite the substantial number of clicks and views needed to keep a sustainable customer base. You may need to come up with your own ideas from time to time to get new customers for yourself.

Fiverr's algorithms and policies are quite dynamic and they will keep on changing, preferably in favor of the buyer. We cannot blame Fiverr for it; they want to be number one among other freelancing platforms and will keep on looking at ways to enhance the quality of deliverables. That is why a lot of successful sellers have been weeded out over the years because they could not keep up with the quality parameters set by Fiverr.

One of the main secrets to being a successful seller on Fiverr is to have a permanent base of clients. These clients will continuously order from you once they have gained your trust. They will not bother about your levels or metrics because they have seen your work and it suits them. Like I said, I have been in situations where my levels kept on fluctuating but that did not affect my sales because of my permanent clients who were there to bail me out every time.

So my advice is, don't become a hostage to Fiverr's levels, metrics or algorithms. Look for ways to build your own client base and establish such a rapport with them, that they continuously return to your for their needs. This will ensure a steady and rising income for you on Fiverr. Never ever bother your clients for ratings; as long as they are giving you orders, you should be happy. I have a client who has placed 40 orders with me but till date she has rated me only on two orders. Doesn't matter, as long as the business keeps coming, I am golden.

I know my shortcomings. I am not one of the best video editors around, there are others who are way more skilled and offer their services far cheaper than me. However, I succeeded because I was able to up sell my work and I was not only dependent upon Fiverr to get clients for me. I put in my fair share of effort to generate clients, they in turned registered with Fiverr to become permanent buyers, thus creating a win win situation for both Fiverr and myself.

Again, I am no super woman; I did not do all the work. I took help of my family to implement these ideas. It required a fair amount of effort and time and I am grateful that my family members stepped up and helped me. You too will require the support of your friends and family in order to implement these ideas. Be shameless; ask anybody and everybody for help. You need to get over your own inhibitions if you want to succeed. Trust me, these ideas will work for you and they will be very effective in skyrocketing your business. By applying these 5 methods and then creating a good working relationship, you too will be able to build a loyal client base.

1.) Chain Mail marketing with email database

The first thing that I tried was to lure buyers to my gigs via email offers. One of my gigs that I offered is "animated logo intros". Here is a screenshot of my gig.

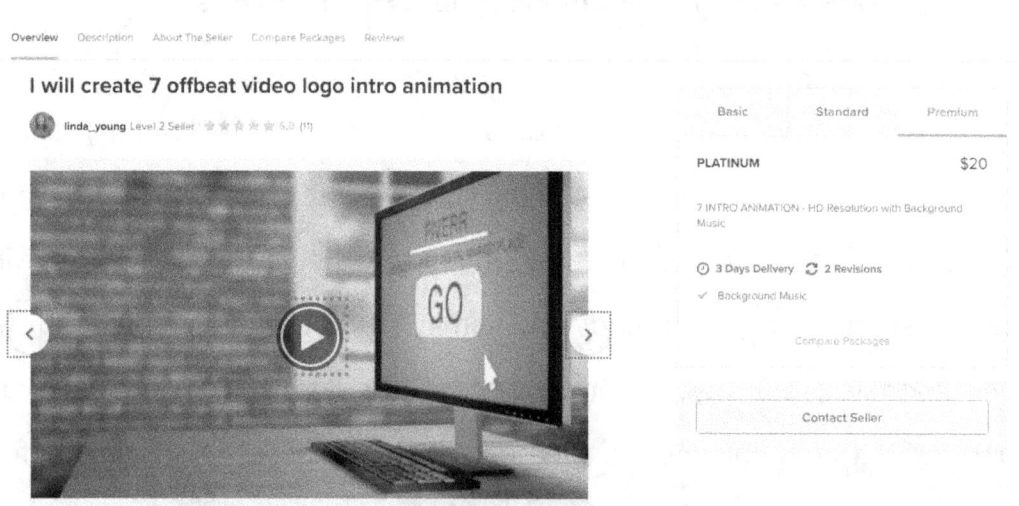

The Premium package of my gig is priced at $20. I wrote a mail in which I added a link of this gig and then offered a onetime discount of 50% on the premium package. I asked people to visit my gig and then send me a message to give a customized offer with a pass code "LIN50". It sounds cheesy but it was mighty effective. Very soon I started getting request for custom offers in anticipation of a discount. Now people could get 7 animations done for $10. This was an offer which was too good to resist because businesses are looking at lot of ways to advertise themselves and if they get 7 short videos to advertise their brand, they will jump on it. This scheme was a hit and I attained a lot of clients with this method.

I took the help of my family members to make the scheme successful. The first thing they did was to scope Facebook, LinkedIn and all social media platforms to build an email database specific to their industry or job type. Once the database was ready, I started sending emails ONE BY ONE to each person addressing him by his name and industry and how this gig would benefit him. Remember, the idea is not to spam email accounts by doing a copy paste job. It will only end up in the Junk folder. While the body of the email can remain the same, you should send the email to each contact separately by addressing his name and industry so that it looks like you have personally contacted him.

The discount feature should be used only once and do not make it a habit to offer discounts repeatedly to your clients. You can bargain for a price which is mutually acceptable to both you and the buyer. This is important, because if the buyer starts coming repeatedly to you, you will find it difficult to demand a higher price at a later stage. So these are the steps you need to follow to retain the buyer permanently.

a.) Lure the buyer with an attractive discount and then complete the order to your buyer's satisfaction.

b.) If the buyer wants a similar service again for the same price, do not agree to it. Explain to him patiently that this was a onetime offer and you cannot afford to offer this service again at that price.

c.) The idea is that the buyer should feel that he is victorious in the negotiation. Offer him a regular discount, let's say 20% and close the deal. Remember, this price has now become permanent in the buyer's mind and every time he orders from you, he will know that he is getting this price. This is how you have attained a permanent buyer for yourself.

2.) Referral Marketing with other Fiverr Sellers

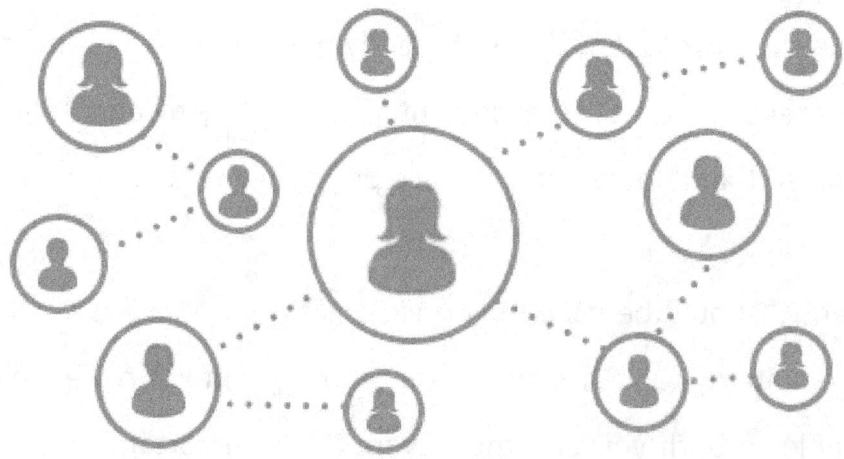

Before I get into this, I want you to know the difference between a lead and a referral. A referral is where someone directs one person who has a particular expertise to another who needs that expertise. We can think of a referral as a qualified sales opportunity where the two parties are introduced to each other and both have agreed to be introduced. Consent is a prime aspect in successful referrals.

A lead is unqualified. It's a chance opportunity with potential. Leads are not personal introductions made by a third party for the mutual benefit of both. A person who is given a lead has no assurance that things will pan out. The lead had not given permission to be contacted, so it's a basic cold call.

Unlike leads, referrals are targeted. A referral is someone who needs what you do, who fits your client profile. There is greater potential for work from referrals than from leads. Referrals generally come to you, while leads are something you chase after.

This scheme will come into play once you have made substantial sales in Fiverr and have built a certain amount of client database. The number is subjective but you should have minimum 50 odd clients for this to work. Now Fiverr has a forum in which sellers come and share their experiences and also take advice on problems that they are dealing with. Here is a screenshot of the forum.

This forum is a good way to interact with other sellers on Fiverr and build your network. Networking within Fiverr is important because it can get you high value clients. Remember, every successful seller on Fiverr offers something unique which is different from others. If you are able to establish a rapport with 10-15 successful sellers, you can generate very good business among yourselves by passing referrals to each other. Let me give you some examples.

I am into video creation and editing and I get all sorts of work such as promotional videos, slideshows, event videos, editing interviews and other content, subtitling work etc. Now let us say someone wants me to add a voice over to his video. I don't provide the service so I refer that buyer to the seller who is providing voiceovers. Similarly, someone wants me to design a logo for their company before creating a branding video. I don't design logos so I refer the buyer to a seller that does the job. One of my gigs is Whiteboard videos and I have buyers who have approached me to design custom images for them. I don't do custom images so I refer the buyer to a graphic artist.

I have made a habit to have a conversation with all my buyers to see if they need help with anything else while I am working on their project. Most of the times, buyers are looking for additional services and if it is out of my scope, I always refer them to other sellers on Fiverr. Once I do that, I contact the seller and let him know about the buyer and his needs. This way I have established a good working relationship with both the buyer as well as the seller. Now you must be wondering, what am I gaining out of this whole exercise? Well, let me fill you in on a little secret about networking.

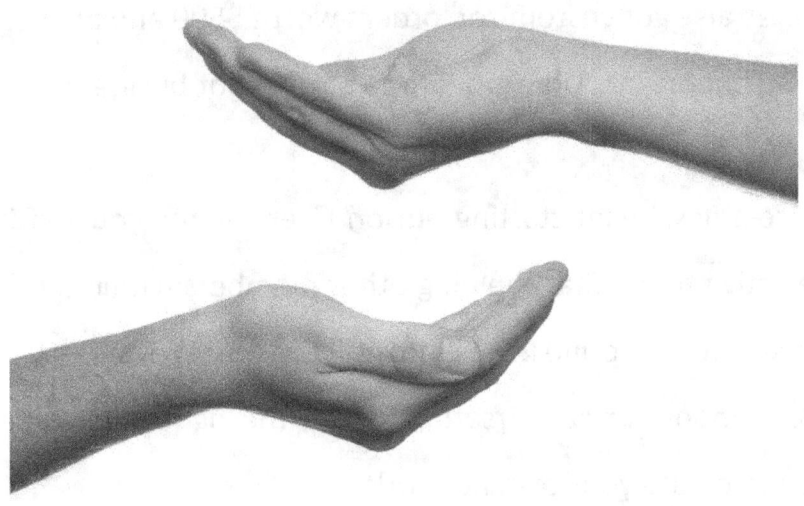

Networking works only if you GIVE MORE than what you receive. This is true with every successful networker. Once you start referring clients to your network, you automatically start raising your credibility as well as your own net worth. You are referring a client who has placed an order with you. So this referral is authentic and if the other seller doesn't mess up, it will 100% convert into an order. Sellers will start taking your referrals seriously. Your buyers will start taking you more seriously because you have been professional in referring a good seller to them.

Nobody wants to feel obligated; it's a simple human emotion. Successful sellers will not be taking favors from you all the time, at some point they will like to return it. This is what happened with me. I started getting referrals from other sellers. Till date I have converted all my referrals into orders.

Referrals are not a volume game like leads. You will get very few referrals within your network. However, unlike leads, these referrals will be 100% authentic and more likely to be converted into a sale. The referrals that I got were few but very high in quality. My average selling price on Fiverr is $56 but with these referrals I got customized orders worth $500 and above. That is why referrals are so important. They guarantee a sure shot business.

Even if you are a new seller starting out on Fiverr, enroll yourself in the forum and become active there. Start helping other members within the forum, make yourself visible. Spend around 20 minutes on the forum every day and try to be a part of every important conversation. When the right time comes, it will be easier for you to create your own network.

3.) Social Shout Outs

Before we expand further on this point, I want you to understand what influencer marketing is? Influencer marketing is a form of collaboration in which an influential person promotes your business. It could be a product, service or a campaign. Celebrity endorsements were the original form of influencer marketing (remember those annoying cola ads promoted by film stars and cricketers). However, in today's digital world, social content creators with niche audiences offer more value to brands. These people have dedicated and engaged groups of followers on social media. They are known as "social media influencers."

Now this method mainly works for gigs that are high in value. A social media influencer has a lot of followers. He could be popular on Youtube, Instagram, Twitter or he could also be running a highly successful blog with a lot of viewers. Depend on the genre of your service; you can decide which influencer will be apt to promote your Fiverr gig.

If you are selling services in $5-$50 range, it will not work for you. The higher the price of your gig, the more likely its chances is of succeeding. This is because working with influencers comes at a cost. It may be in the form of paying something upfront or giving them an affiliate commission. This method can also work for services you are offering beyond Fiverr. Let me explain how.

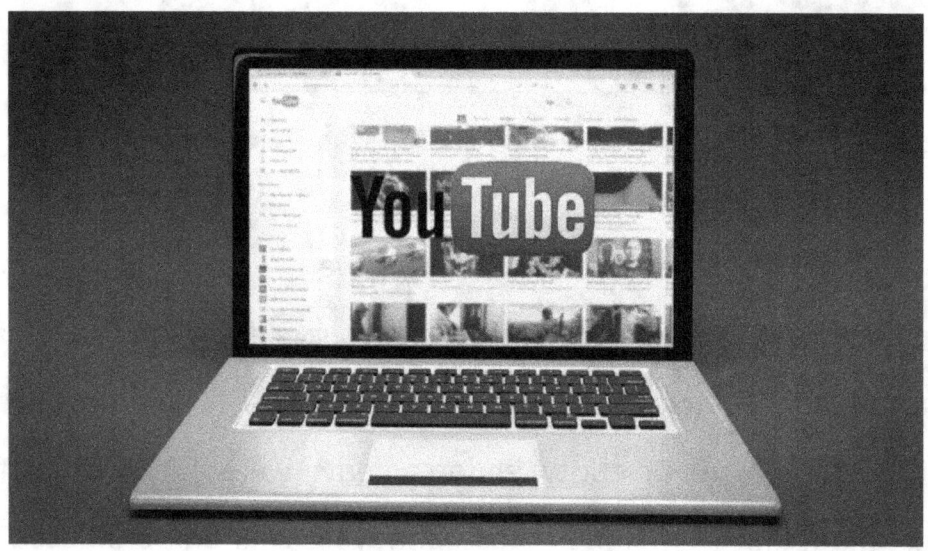

I edit videos for a lot of clients who are running their YouTube channels. Some of these channels are quite popular and have a good number of subscribers. Over a period of time after having worked a lot with my clients, I started asking them for small favors such as promoting my gigs in their channels to derive more sales. My clients responded positively and gave a shout out to their followers to come and check out my gigs. Due to this exercise I managed to get a few orders. This was my first introduction to influencer marketing. I realized that it works. However with Fiverr, I knew I would have limitations in getting the attention of real influencers. Most of my gigs don't command a very high price. I also did not want to do anything that could violate Fiverr's policies.

I then decided to create my own portfolio. A family member creating my portfolio on "wixsite" in which I embedded the YouTube links of a few videos that I had created for my clients. Once the portfolio was ready, I decided to seek out an Influencer.

One of my specialties is slideshow videos which cover events like birthdays, festivals, travel etc. We contacted someone who is popular in Instagram for posting her travel pics and she had a sizeable number of followers. I offered to make "30 seconds" slideshow videos for her every day for free. All she had to do was to acknowledge who created this video and then give the link to my portfolio. I also made a sample video from her Instagram images and showed it to her. She was happy with the video and decided to experiment with me for 15 days. So for 15 days she would share a new slideshow video every day and then give a shout out pointing to my portfolio. The scheme worked and a lot of people approached me to create slideshow videos for personal and professional events. I was able to generate good business out of this scheme.

I am not using this method anymore because I am already swamped with orders from Fiverr. However, I know this scheme works and it is highly effective. As I mentioned before, this method will work for those high priced gigs which involves a lot of work quality such as high end graphics, video marketing, digital marketing and website / app creations and so on. You can pay the Influencer either in the form of free service, upfront amount or affiliate commission. You need to figure out the payment structure. Having an Influencer endorsing your work also lends credibility to your gig.

4.) Get people to promote your gigs for a commission

This has been by far the most effective way in getting new buyers for my gigs. The best part about this method is that I have paid zero commission to people who have promoted my gigs. Instead, they have been compensated by Fiverr, as much as $15 to $50 per gig. Surprised? Let me explain how.

Fiverr is right now running a very successful campaign known as the "Affiliate Commission Program". You can join this program and start earning commission by referring Fiverr's gigs and other services to prospective buyers. Anybody can join the program and you don't even need to have a website which is a requirement for most affiliate programs.

Fiverr has a different commission structure for all gigs. The highest is $50 per gig and following categories pay for this commission:

1.) Whiteboard & Animated Explainers

Video & Animation

2.) Book & eBook Writing - NEW!

Writing & Translation

3.) Architecture & Interior Design - NEW!

Graphics & Design

4.) Game Development

Programming & Tech

I have two gigs that are under the category of whiteboard and animated explainers. That means if somebody refers a buyer to my gig, he will be paid a commission of $50 from Fiverr. Not bad huh? I have taken maximum advantage of this scheme. The first thing that I did was to circulate and advertise this scheme among my immediate network of friends, family and colleagues. My family and i advertised this scheme in our Whatsapp groups, business groups, LinkedIn contacts etc. to enroll people to register for this scheme. Very soon we had around 25-30 people who had registered as Fiverr affiliates and these people started promoting my gigs on their blogs, website and social media platforms. They were able to generate first time buyers and earn a side hustle while I benefited by getting more traffic to my gig.

Even today I make it a point to add at least one or two affiliates every month. As you are reading this lesson, I will advise you to become an affiliate as well. Start promoting my gigs and earn $50 each time a buyer buys my gig (ha ha, just kidding). But on a serious note, "Fiverr Affiliates" is a very powerful program. You will definitely earn something if you enroll in it. All the links that an affiliate is provided with, include a 12 month tracking cookie. If someone clicks on your link and does not buy anything immediately but after 6 months, you will still get a commission for that order. Apart from gigs, there are a lot of other Fiverr services too that you can sell and some of them have commissions as high as $150. If you take the approach of promoting Fiverr seriously, you can easily make $1000 and above every month from this scheme alone.

5.) Reward your new customers with offers to retain their loyalty

Over a period of time, once you have dealt with different customers, you will want some of them to keep coming back to you to order your gigs. I am very picky about repeat customers but once I have made up my mind about a certain client, I go all out to retain him. One of the features that I contently use to retain a customer is the "Fiverr Anywhere" Program. This feature is especially useful for a new seller or a number one seller who is looking to quickly scale those levels. Let me explain this program in brief.

Using 'Fiverr Anywhere' for Sending Custom Offers

"Fiverr Anywhere" is a feature that allows you to create a customer offer for your gig and then a link is generated which you can share with anyone or anywhere across websites, blogs or social media platforms. The useful thing about this offer is that it can be valid for a long as 30 days. So in a way, it becomes a valid coupon code or offer which the buyer can use within 30 days.

As stated earlier, I am very choosy on repeat customers. I use this feature effectively only for those clients with whom I am interested in gaining their loyalty. So, for instance, a buyer placed an order for my video editing gig. I had a good experience working with him and I want him to order from me again. I also want to showcase my other gigs to him, let us say, the whiteboard animation gig? So what do I do? I create an attractive offer for him through

"Fiverr Anywhere" and share the link while delivering his order. When he clicks the link, this is what the customer offer will look like.

Review Your Order
Please review your order before checkout

I will create a two minutes whiteboard video for only $10. All I need from you is a a script and voice over (if any). I will use images and clip arts sourced from google and my software to create a storyboard. For custom images or any other specific you may contact me and I will make a new offer suited to your needs.

linda_young

★ ★ ★ ★ ★ (by 141 users)
Joined Fiverr over 3 years ago

Duration: 5 days
Expiration: May 24, 20

Total $10.0

Proceed to payment

Now my offer is valid for 30 days. It is a discounted offer of 50% because this service costs $20 in the main gig. What I have done here is to generate an interest in the buyer to either order from this gig or at the very least, take a look at this gig along with my other gigs. This ploy has worked for me majorly, whenever I have chosen to do so.

If you are a new seller, this is a very effective way to keep your buyer interested. If he has ordered your gig for the first time, make another offer (albeit an attractive one) and provide him the link after your existing order has been successfully completed. Trust me, this will work wonders for you.

Concluding Summary

I want to congratulate and thank you for your patience and diligence applied in completing this book. You are ready to lead the lifestyle of a successful entrepreneur. Before I wind up, I want to share a few things that you must adopt in your daily routine so that you do not exhaust yourself or burnout in the quest of being a successful freelancer.

I want you to succeed and use Fiverr in every possible way. Create a positive environment for yourself while pursuing your freelancing career. Get yourself an organized, dedicated workplace. It could be anything, a desk in an office, a coffee shop or even a couch in your living room. It's critical to keep your surroundings in order to have a comfortable and productive workspace. You should treat this workspace as your office. Remove clutter, personal items and other things that may distract you in your workspace. Put a premium on you time that you are devoting here. Set comfortable work hours so that you can manage your customer's expectations. Don't be greedy, do not worry about the money, it will come. You first need to figure out how much you can stretch yourself while delivering to your client's needs.

Do not make yourself available 24/7. You will wear yourself thin and your work will suffer. Make sure to let your customers know when you can be contacted and when you can get back to them. To be healthy and happy you need a social life as well, so keep your work life in balance.

Even though it may sound silly, dress yourself appropriately before you come to your workspace. Like I said before, treat the workspace as your office. You will be inspired to work harder and smarter if you have a work uniform. It doesn't have to be anything formal, just something professional to put you in the mood for work. Avoid using pirated software. Make sure that all your work related software is up to date so that you can avoid any customer conflict in which your tools are not compatible with file formats they have sent.

Fiverr is a marketplace that continues to grow and succeed because talented sellers are catering to clients all over the world on a daily basis. Due to this continuous growth and innovation, Fiverr continues to create opportunities for sellers to earn serious money.

So let us go through a short summary of all the main points we have covered so far ....

1.) You must optimize your seller profile and empower your gigs with killer description and images that convert leads into sales.
2.) You can set your prices and put together packages and extras that will generate higher sales.
3.) Maintain strong communication with your customer and use the tools Fiverr has to up sell your work.
4.) Promote your Fiverr account aggressively on social media.
5.) Be mindful of Fiverr metrics and make sure to maintain 5 star ratings across all parameters consistently to rise up in levels.

You are now set to live the life of a successful freelancer. Command your own space and keep work-life balance that works for you. Make sure to keep on revisiting this eBook and refresh your memory with the best practices you have learnt from it. As a Fiverr seller, you are here to do amazing things.

www.ingramcontent.com/pod-product-compliance
Lightning Source LLC
Chambersburg PA
CBHW080925220526
45465CB00008BA/2941